Breakthrough Devotional is the project of Rev. Dr. Jeff Dorman who has served as a GiANT consultant and guide since 2013. It was developed with the knowledge and blessing of GiANT leadership but is not an official company product of GiANT Worldwide or GiANT.TV.

A DEVOTIONAL COMPANION TO GIANT'S *INVINCIBLE* SYSTEM

BREAK THROUGH

UNLOCK YOUR POTENTIAL

Dr. Jeffrey S. Dorman

HIGH BRIDGE BOOKS
HOUSTON

Breakthrough
by Dr. Jeffrey S. Dorman

Printed in the United States of America
ISBN: 978-1-954943-03-2

High Bridge Books titles may be purchased in bulk for educational, business, fundraising, or sales promotional use. For information, please contact High Bridge Books via www.HighBridgeBooks.com/contact.

Published in Houston, Texas by High Bridge Books

Contents

Introduction

Josh landed his first prominent leadership position at age 34. He lived in the heartland of America and worked in a small division of a large corporation. Although well educated, Josh realized he had much more to learn. This opportunity made him hungry for success and want his team to succeed. Josh knew he and his team were good enough, but he wanted a breakthrough that would make them exemplary.

Josh heard how the practical tools and proven GiANT Worldwide principles could make teams highly effective. The new *Invincible* program appeared to be just the ticket for him. Using the online video resources and worksheets with his team, Josh understood his teammates' "Voice" tendencies and himself. This revelation raised their communication, understanding, and decision-making to a whole new level. As the year unfolded, this team worked through the 50 Sherpa training sessions and raised their productivity by over 20%. Thanks to *Invincible,* Josh became a company hero. Even more valuable, Josh developed into a healthier man, a quality leader, and a better husband and father.

Unknown to his colleagues, Josh drew from an additional source of power in the form of his *Breakthrough* devotional companion for the *Invincible* system. The Scripture, devotional, and prayer integrated with each session helped unleash the power of his faith. The synergy of personal faith and insightful principles fueled his personal and professional growth and empowered the breakthrough he had been seeking!

Individuals and teams are improving all over the USA and in over 116 other countries as businesses and organizations are discovering the benefits of creating *Invincible* teams through GiANT.TV/success. The *Breakthrough* devotional companion bridges the Sunday to Monday gap for Christians.

As a pastor for over 20 years, I know the power of unleashing faith alongside quality development principles. Women and men like Josh working in the secular world can use this book in the privacy of their homes and boost their training through the integrated Scripture, devotional, and prayer for each session.

Christian churches, colleges, and non-profits will benefit by using Breakthrough *alongside* Invincible *with their staff, faculty, boards, or groups of their members or students. This program enhanced our lives and transformed our ministry.*

—Jim and Martha Brangenberg, Talk Show Hosts @ iWork4Him

Breakthrough connects our Christian faith with one of the best human development opportunities available. *Invincible* "unlocks the potential of people," and *Breakthrough* unites those practical principles with the power of God, resulting in a transformational experience.

When does 4+4=16? When you turn the plus into a multiplication sign. When you multiply the *Invincible* principles by faith, remarkable (dare I say miraculous?) things can happen in an individual, a team, or an organization.

In nearly a decade of teaching GiANT principles and tools, time and again, I heard these words: "What an excellent experience. I wish I had learned this 20 years ago! Then I (and those around me) would have been so much better off." Hearing people express such regret fuels my passion for lifting the next generation on our shoulders. I'm devoting the rest of my career to helping them be the healthiest, happiest, and most productive generation the world has ever seen.

What You Will Find in *Breakthrough*

- Inspirational Bible passages
- Motivating readings
- Uplifting prayers
- Collect your Breakthrough Journal insights
- Questions for reflection or group discussion

The book's 51 sections correlate with the orientation and 50 sessions of *Invincible.*

The rhythm of each week follows this pattern:

- ***Invited***: Scripture, devotional, and prayer set the scene for the learning opportunity.
- ***Invincible***: Watch the video, then complete the 100 Exercise and the X Challenge.
- ***Involved***: Scripture, devotional, and prayer will activate your new learning.
- ***Invested***: A) Write a vital insight in your journal, then B) reflect on or discuss your learning and action items with your group.

What Kind of Breakthrough Are You Seeking?

- To communicate effectively with everyone you lead
- To be present and productive when there is never enough time
- To get unstuck and move up to the next level

- To become someone worth following
- To increase your influence
- To build an unbeatable team
- To establish a healthy organizational culture

I believe using this devotional with the *Invincible* system will provide a breakthrough for you!

Orientation

Invited

> *After [Paul, Barnabas, and a few others] were sent off and on their way, they told everyone they met as they traveled through Phoenicia and Samaria about the breakthrough to the non-Jewish outsiders. Everyone who heard the news cheered—it was terrific news!*
>
> —Acts 15:3 MSG

> *...[King David] said, "The* Lord *has broken through my enemies before me, like a breakthrough of water." So he named that place Baal-perazim (master of breakthroughs).*
>
> —2 Samuel 5:20b AMP

An amazing discovery or a tremendous amount of progress can be called a breakthrough. For example, a personal breakthrough might be overcoming your fear of public speaking or changing your lifestyle and losing that extra 40 pounds.

The twentieth-century produced hundreds of societal breakthroughs, including improvements such as:

- the shift from flames to electric lightbulbs as a source of light
- the change from horses to automobiles as the primary mode of transportation
- the discovery of penicillin in 1928 as a breakthrough for modern medicine

Breakthroughs might be:

- a sudden, dramatic, and important discovery or development
- penetration of a barrier, such as an enemy's defense
- an instance of achieving success in a particular sphere or activity

Let's take a look at the two breakthroughs mentioned in the Scriptures above.

It took a massive breakthrough for the first Christians to shift from believing that Jesus came only for the Jews to recognize the Spirit of God was poured out upon Gentiles (non-Jews). All people could now experience God's love, forgiveness, and salvation through Jesus Christ. This dramatic shift upended the early Church and established Christianity's course, so the message spread across the earth.

King David experienced a victory in battle over the Philistines, described as God breaking through the enemies before him. He experienced God that day as "Lord of breakthroughs."

What about you? What kind of breakthrough do you need?

- A mind-shift toward new principles and tools?
- Breaking out from internal and external barriers that hinder you?
- Empowerment to achieve success at a higher level?

Take a moment and think about your desired breakthroughs. In fact, how about beginning a Breakthrough journal (or document on your computer)? Each week you choose a breakthrough concept or insight from the session, and at the end of the year, you will have collected 50 empowering discoveries. Then celebrate the ones you have implemented and set a strategy for using the rest.

You are not in this devotional book or the *Invincible* training by accident. Expect God will meet your needs, transform your life, and give you breakthroughs on many levels. Raise your hope, your expectations, and your faith.

Lord Jesus, open my mind to receive all you have for me in today's video sessions. Open my ears to hear your voice in my heart. Open my eyes to see the summit where I will behold the glories of your Kingdom. Amen.

Invincible

- Complete the Sherpa Training Session 0: Orientation
- Video, 100 Exercise, and X Challenge

Involved

> *I praise you [O Lord] because I am fearfully and wonderfully made; your works are wonderful, I know that full well.*
>
> —Psalm 139:14 NIV

Many people read this verse and think, "It may work for the Psalmist and maybe for others, but it is not my experience!" At one time or another in their lives, many feel burned out, beat up, or merely bored, wondering, "Is that all there is?" Some feel trapped in a stressful job that leaves them unhappy and unsatisfied. Others question if they are fulfilling their life's purpose. Have you ever felt this way? If so, you are not alone.

In the same way that musicians must make music, poets must write, and artists must paint, we all have unique gifts designed for a specific contribution that will bring meaning and purpose to our lives. Real joy and happiness will elude us until we use our gifts and become who God created us to be.

You are using your gifts when:

- you feel energized by your work,
- you can't wait to get up and get going in the morning,
- your contribution makes a difference and gives you satisfaction, and
- you find your activities life-giving!

As you contemplate the *70/30 Principle* this week (and throughout the coming year), ask God for revelation about your gifts, passions, and purpose. Take steps that invest 70% of your energy operating in the strengths God has given you.

Lord God, help me recognize who you created me to be. Let my heart believe I, too, am "wonderfully made." Grant me opportunities to know my gifts, strengths, and passions so I might bless others by using them at work, at home, and in the community. Help my self-identity and life functions line up with how you created me.

Be glorified as you release my God-given strengths and competence to bless others around me. Energize me to make a difference! Amen.

Invested

A. Please identify your vital insight from this session and write it in your *Breakthrough* Journal.

B. For reflection or discussion:

1. David experienced God as "Lord of Breakthroughs." What breakthrough do you need from God this year?
2. What might keep you from believing you are "wonderfully made" by God? What would change for you if you profoundly believed this?
3. What gives you life? What are some natural strengths you would like to use 70% of the time?
4. What is draining for you? What are some challenging functions you would appreciate reducing to 30%?
5. Is your 70:30 in balance? Why or why not?
6. What three changes might move you toward a healthy 70:30?

7. If the goal is not conquering the mountain but rather conquering yourself, what personal breakthrough would you ask God for this year?
8. What mind-shift or discovery would be helpful?
9. What barriers have hindered you?
10. What would empower you to achieve greater success?
11. Who is counting on your help so they can make the summit?

1

Peace Index and Leadership Baseline

Invited

> *Peace I leave with you; my peace I give you. I do not give to you as the world gives. Do not let your hearts be troubled and do not be afraid.*
>
> —John 14:27 NIV

The typical western definition of peace is the absence of conflict or war. But in Hebrew, the word "shalom" means so much more.

What does shalom mean biblically?

In the Bible, shalom most commonly refers to a state of well-being, harmony, wholeness, completeness, prosperity, welfare, and tranquility. Using the word shalom as a greeting imparts a blessing—a manifestation of divine grace.

Experiencing Shalom signifies complete well-being—physical, psychological, social, and spiritual. Shalom flows from a threefold relationship of being right with God, with(in) yourself, and with others.

To most of us, this idea of completeness or wholeness seems like the "happily ever after" concept in a fairy tale. We regularly experience challenges, trials, and circumstances that may steal our peace. Today's session includes assessing your level of Peace by considering five different areas of your life.

- **Purpose**: Are you doing what you were "created" to do? Are you *alive* in your work?
- **People**: How healthy are your relationships with family (nuclear and extended), friends, co-workers, neighbors?
- **Place**: How are your surroundings impacting your life, either positively or negatively? Consider such factors as where you live, your town, home, community, and office space.
- **Personal Health**: How do you feel about your health? What are your concerns?
- **Provision**: How do you feel about what you are receiving commensurate to what you are doing?

We'll unpack all of this in today's videos. But let's begin with prayer.

Lord Jesus, messages from the world rob us of peace. But you do not give as the world gives. Guide me today as I consider what changes might help me experience greater peace. Peace with God. Peace with other people. Peace within myself. Reveal your definition of wholeness and completeness. Grant me your peace. Amen.

Invincible

- Complete the Sherpa Training Session 1: Peace Index
- Video, 100 Exercise, and X Challenge

Involved

> *Do not worry about anything, but in everything by prayer and supplication with thanksgiving let your requests be made known to God. And the peace of God, which surpasses all understanding, will guard your hearts and your minds in Christ Jesus.*
>
> —Philippians 4:6–7 NRSV

The Peace Index process today helps us know ourselves a little bit better. We will require God's help to not be anxious and live in profound peace. Ask God to:

Reveal what outer elements (circumstances, situations, relationships, etc.) must change to gain peace.

Disclose what inner workings (in our thinking and attitudes) should change to experience peace.

Teach us to lay down those things causing anxiousness and practice, giving all of our cares to the One who cares for us.

Empower us to:

1. live with no regrets because the blood of Jesus cleansed our yesterdays,
2. live with no worries because our tomorrows are safe in the hands of our merciful God, and
3. live fully alive and today in the fellowship with the Holy Spirit.

May the peace of God guard our hearts and minds in Christ Jesus.

God grant me the Serenity
To accept the things I cannot change,
Courage to change the things I can,
And the Wisdom to know the difference. Amen.
—Reinhold Niebuhr

Invested

A. Please identify your vital insight from this session and write it in your *Breakthrough* Journal.

B. For reflection or discussion:

1. How might you experience more biblical shalom?
2. Purpose: Are you doing what you were "created" to do? Are you *alive* in your work?
3. People: How healthy are your relationships with family (nuclear and extended), friends, co-workers, and neighbors?
4. Place: How are your surroundings impacting your life, either positively or negatively? Consider such factors as where you live, your town, home, community, and office space.
5. Personal Health: How do you feel about your health? What are your concerns?
6. Provision: How do you feel about what you are receiving commensurate to what you are doing?
7. Which of the five areas will you improve to raise your peace index significantly?
8. What things cause you concern and anxiousness?

9. How could your thinking and attitudes change from being anxious to experiencing peace?
10. What might eliminate any regrets from the past or worries about the future?

2

Support/Challenge with Family and Team

Invited

> *...speaking the truth in love, we will grow to become in every respect the mature body of him who is the head, that is, Christ.*
>
> —Ephesians 4:15 NIV

Truth without love can be harsh, demanding, and even damaging to those around us. Love without truth may be misleading and insincere. Yet truth and love are not enemies to be reconciled but companions to welcome as one. Healthy relationships require both truth and love. For healthy growth, humans need support and challenge, encouragement and accountability, love and truth.

Most people are good at one side of this equation and have a blind spot where they fail at the other. Understanding our strengths and weakness in this essential paradox is crucial. The goal remains to become a person who calibrates *both* support and challenge (love and truth) toward ourselves, our families, our team, and beyond.

Lord Jesus, let me grow in you. Let me be more like you. Show me how to integrate truth and love, so I support and challenge those I lead. Thank you.

Invincible

- Complete the Sherpa Training Session 2: Support and Challenge
- Video, 100 Exercise, and X Challenge

Involved

> *Whatever you wish that others would do to you, do also to them, for this is the Law and the Prophets.*
>
> —Matthew 7:12 ESV

The Golden Rule principle necessitates treating others as you would like them to treat you. Why call it golden? Because of the tremendous value in having this kind of respect and caring attitude for one another.

Please consider these questions (and the others in the reflection/discussion section):

- When I am leading others (and especially when I am under stress), am I treating them as I want to be treated?
- What adjustments would calibrate support and challenge so people will experience me as a liberator?

Lord Jesus, make me neither a tyrant nor a toadstool. Make me an effective leader who calibrates both support and challenge to empower those around me. Reveal how adjusting my thinking, speech, and behavior will make me more like you. Let me repent where my shortcomings have affected others. Empower me to learn, grow, and become more of a Liberator. Remind me every day to treat others as I wish to be treated. Amen.

Invested

A. Please identify your vital insight from this session and write it in your *Breakthrough* Journal.

B. For reflection or discussion:

1. In what situation or relationship did you experience an imbalance of truth and love?
2. Which is more natural for you: giving others truth or love? Why?
3. What shall you adjust (especially when under stress) to treat others as you want them to treat you?
4. What would it mean for you to light a fire within them rather than underneath them?
5. How can you communicate expectations more clearly?
6. How do your family and team experience your leadership?
7. Who might feel you are too harsh and overbearing? Who might think you are wishy-washy and unclear?
8. How shall you calibrate support and challenge, so people experience you as a liberator?

9. What would it look like to provide what others deserve and treat them how you wish to be treated?
10. How would one relationship improve if you apply more of the golden rule?

3

Liberate Yourself

Invited

To liberate yourself or others, first overcome the universal barrier: *fear*. We must conquer the primal human experience of fear to develop into all God desires for us. This fear may be present because of a combination of nature, nurture, and choice, and because the Enemy controls people through fear. Whatever the origin, people must overcome fear to Liberate others.

In the business world, those who naturally dominate are often afraid and say, "People won't be productive enough if I am too nice." People act out of fear when they use bullying and manipulation as "motivation" for others to get things done. This dominant behavior damages individuals and organizations.

People who protect are either afraid somebody won't like them if they bring challenges or fear challenge will damage the team dynamic they wish to achieve. But protector behavior stifles, limits, and hinders growth in others. Love does not avoid challenging others.

People who abdicate are often paralyzed by fear and frozen like deer staring into the headlights of an oncoming car on the highway.

To liberate yourself or others, you must intentionally work to overcome fear.

Since there are around 365 references in the Bible related to the concepts of "do not be afraid," you might say God provides one "fear not" verse for every day of the year. This theme in the Bible challenges us to love and trust God and not be afraid. Consider a few examples.

> *The* LORD *himself goes before you and will be with you; he will never leave you nor forsake you. Do not be afraid; do not be discouraged.*
>
> —Deuteronomy 31:8 NIV

> *Do not fear, for I have redeemed you; I have called you by name; you are mine.*
>
> —Isaiah 43:1b NIV

> *Be strong and courageous. Do not be afraid; do not be discouraged, for the* LORD *your God will be with you wherever you go.*
>
> —Joshua 1:9 NIV

> *So do not fear, for I am with you; do not be dismayed, for I am your God. I will strengthen you and help you; I will uphold you with my righteous right hand.*
>
> —Isaiah 41:10 NIV

As you consider today how God would have you liberate yourself, you may want to begin with the following prayer.

Lord Jesus, I know your power sets me free, and your freedom includes freedom from fear. Grant me freedom from any protecting, dominating, or abdicating thoughts, self-talk, or behaviors toward myself. Reveal the roots of my fear and help me cast fear down by trusting in your promises, your provision, and your presence. Show me today how liberating myself is part of your plan for my personal growth and maturity. Amen.

Invincible

- Complete the Sherpa Training Session 3: Support and Challenge for Yourself
- Video, 100 Exercise, and X Challenge

Involved

> *There is no fear in love. But perfect love drives out fear, because fear has to do with punishment. The one who fears is not made perfect in love.*
>
> —1 John 4:18 NIV

After hearing this verse in Sunday school, a child asked his mom, "How could love fight fear?"

At first, the parent felt stumped. Verses like this can be vague and difficult to grasp, even for adults. But when meditating on this scripture and how God's love has made her less fearful through life, one explanation became evident.

God is love. Perfect love. And the closer we come toward God, the less power fear has over us because we feel God's continual presence, strength, comfort, and guidance.

This concept reminded her of being a child and experiencing "scary" situations, like hearing a strange noise in the middle of the night. She remembered yelling for her dad, feeling terrified, but having a total belief her dad would protect her.

When faced with crippling fear, trust God with the confidence a child ascribes to a loving parent. The key is abiding in love on a moment by moment basis. Love is not merely a biblical idea. God invites us to experience love continually so that it becomes experiential truth in our lives.

Jesus made love the centerpiece of life. He declared the greatest commandment is: "Love the Lord your God with all your heart and with all your soul and with all your mind." And he quickly added the second most important thing: *"Love your neighbor as yourself"* (Matt. 22:38-39 NIV).

Lord God, I realize there are times and situations in which I have been too hard on myself (dominating). Other times, I have avoided accountability and coddled myself (protecting). Sometimes I have opted out and avoided responsibility (abdicating). These examples of poor self-leadership often arise out of fear, but you call me to love. Take away my fear as I experience your love more and more every day. Fill my heart with love for you, for others, and for myself. Loving myself means calibrating self-support and self-challenge. Then, empowered by your Spirit, I will think *appropriate thoughts,* hold *suitable attitudes, and* do *the right things. May it be so. Amen.*

Invested

A. Please identify your vital insight from this session and write it in your *Breakthrough* Journal.

B. For reflection or discussion:

1. When you are out of balance concerning support and challenge, what is your natural tendency (protect, dominate, or abdicate)? Give an example.
2. What fear might be behind that tendency?
3. What biblical concept, promise, or truth may help you conquer your fear?
4. What does abiding in God's love mean to you?

5. When is one time you experienced abiding in God's love?
6. Where have you sometimes failed yourself by 1) being too hard on yourself, 2) letting yourself off the hook and coddling yourself, or 3) opting out and avoiding?
7. How would providing support and challenge for yourself be loving?
8. How might you better provide support and challenge for others by offering these behaviors to yourself?
9. What does it mean to "properly" love yourself?
10. What will empower you to *think* appropriate thoughts, *hold* beneficial attitudes, and *do* the right things, more support or more challenge?

4

The 5 Circles of Influence

Invited

> *The good influence of godly citizens causes a city to prosper, but the moral decay of the wicked drives it downhill.*
>
> —Proverbs 11:11 TLB

We could expand the application of this verse and say, "The good influence of a godly person causes blessings that make things flourish, thrive, grow and succeed in the five circles of the person's influence."

1. Self: our personal lives
2. Family: those we love, with whom we have the highest commitment
3. Team: the 3–10 people with whom we work most closely

4. Organization: the ripple effects of our work into the larger organization
5. Community: our relationships and activities in the neighborhood, church, and civic organizations

What are the ways you can see God's blessings flowing through your life? What would it mean to be more intentional about having a positive influence in each of these areas? These are the questions we will be looking at today.

Lord Jesus, I don't want my life bouncing around like a ball in a pinball machine. I want my life to count for you—at home, at work, and in the community. Show me today how intentional godly living can release your blessings to those around me. Make me a blessing to someone today. Amen.

Invincible

- Complete the Sherpa Training Session 4: 5 Circles of Influence
- Video, 100 Exercise, and X Challenge

Involved

> *Only if you return to trusting me will I let you continue as my spokesman. You are to influence them, not let them influence you! They will fight against you like a besieging army against a high city wall. But they will not conquer you, for I am with you to protect and deliver you, says the Lord.*
>
> —Jeremiah 15:19b–20 TLB

In this passage, God encourages Jeremiah to fulfill his calling, make a difference, and trust that the Lord would protect and deliver him even when facing significant opposition. Jeremiah's situation may seem a bit larger than the struggles of your daily life, so let's ask a more straightforward question:

Are you a thermometer or a thermostat?

A thermometer reveals the temperature in the room, while a thermostat *sets* the temperature in the room. One is influenced by its surroundings while the other influences its surroundings. Here's the challenge:

You are to influence them, not let them influence you!

A human thermometer is intentional in all 5 Circles of Influence, trusting the Lord's goodness and righteousness to shine from our lives. We count on the Lord's protection and deliverance when facing either seemingly impossible or easy challenges of life.

God, make me an influencer that sets the temperature of the room. Let blessings flow through me to those around me. Empower me to live intentionally and purposefully. Use my life for your purposes. Let me be like you in thoughts, attitudes, words, and how I treat the people I encounter. Amen.

For Reflection or Discussion

1. Share an example of a time you saw God's blessings flowing through your life and touch another.
2. How might you be more aware of similar opportunities in the future?

3. What would it mean to be more intentional about positively influencing each of the following areas: self, family, team, organization, and community?
4. Do you tend to function as a thermometer or a thermostat? Share an example.
5. In what settings are you more influenced, and in what settings are you more of an influencer? Share an example.
6. Where in your life or relationships ought you be more intentional rather than accidental?
7. How do you sense God's presence and activity in daily life, at home, at work, and in the community?
8. What is your learning opportunity regarding intentional living?
9. What is your plan for growth?
10. Recount a time when God's blessings were flowing through you to bless others.

5

Know Yourself to Lead Yourself

Invited

> *There is no one righteous, not even one; there is no one who understands…*
>
> —Romans 3:10b–11a NIV

> *…all have sinned and fall short of the glory of God, and all are justified freely by His grace through the redemption that came by Christ Jesus.*
>
> —Romans 3:23–24 NIV

Knowing yourself always precedes leading yourself. And knowing yourself starts with what Alcoholics Anonymous calls "taking a fearless moral inventory." It means looking at yourself in the mirror and being honest about what you see. It also means asking and listening as others who care about you share what you don't see: your blind spots.

We all fall short, and not merely with a few isolated faults or missteps. All human beings have a bent, a propensity, and a tendency toward sinning in some form or another. Following our negative tendencies creates patterns and habits of sin.

Temptation leads to actions that have consequences that damage both our lives and those around us.

Think of it this way: tendencies are not all bad. Some of a person's tendencies lead them to be loving and successful. Some tendencies are benign—they neither help much nor hinder significantly. But for most people, some tendencies impede our personal growth and success while negatively impacting those who encounter us.

No one is righteous, and everyone has blind spots. The first step toward growth is acknowledging those tendencies and patterns that cause problems for ourselves and others. Only then can we receive God's grace and redemptive power to overcome those shortcomings.

Lord, help me to know myself. Reveal my tendencies, patterns, and actions that need attention. Don't let me fool myself any longer. Please show me what you want to change. Amen.

Invincible

- Complete the Sherpa Training Session 5: Know Yourself to Lead Yourself
- Video, 100 Exercise, and X Challenge

Involved

> *From that time on Jesus began to preach, "Repent, for the kingdom of heaven has come near."*
>
> —Matthew 4:17 NIV

The right response to the Good News is simple and profound. All people must repent and believe in the Gospel. But what does Scripture mean by "repent" and "believe?" And how does this connect with knowing yourself to lead yourself?

When Jesus said, "Repent," He was talking about a change of heart toward sin, the world, and God. This inner change produces new ways of living that exalt Christ and give evidence of the Gospel's truth.

What does repenting mean? In the New Testament, the Greek word translated as "repent" is *metanoeo*. It has two parts: *meta* and *noeo*. The second part, *noeo,* refers to your inner self's disposition—your "default setting" toward reality. The first part, *meta,* is a prefix meaning movement or change. *Meta,* or "change," plus *noeo,* or "disposition" equals changing your disposition toward life and reality and embracing a transformed default setting about what's important.

Your tendencies are examples of the disposition of your inner self—your default settings. Some of them will change as you agree with God that they are harmful and work to replace them with the truth revealed through Jesus Christ. Other tendencies seem deeply wired, and you will repeatedly fight the good fight to avoid going down that pathway again.

Also, remember you have not yet discovered all the tendencies that need changing. We never graduate from the school of self-discovery. Gaining self-understanding is a lifelong journey.

The good news is we are not alone in this fight. The Kingdom of heaven has come near. Jesus is present to help us, and the victory He won is available to us. Believe and receive the forgiveness, love, and transformative power of Christ for yourself.

Lord, thank you for revealing the detrimental tendencies that harm me or those around me. Let me overcome old patterns by prayerfully visu-

alizing new pathways. Empower me to choose a better path. Help me change my actions so their consequences will bless others. Amen.

Invested

A. Please identify your vital insight from this session and write it in your *Breakthrough* Journal.

B. For reflection or discussion:

1. Following your "fearless moral inventory," if you are totally honest, what ought to change?
2. We all have blind spots. Who in your life is honest enough to tell you about your blind spots?
3. What area of life requires the transformation of your default setting about what is important?
4. What is one negative tendency that causes problems for you or those around you?
5. What patterns or habits (of thought or words) arise out of this problem tendency?
6. What actions result from those thought patterns?
7. What are the consequences of those actions?
8. How does this affect your reality and how others see you?
9. What tendencies, patterns, habits, attitudes, or actions are the Holy Spirit convicting you to change?
10. What will you put in place to interrupt those tendencies and create healthier patterns of action?

6

Who Says You Can't?

Invited

> *"Have faith in God," Jesus answered. "Truly I tell you, if anyone says to this mountain, 'Go, throw yourself into the sea,' and does not doubt in their heart but believes that what they say will happen, it will be done for them. Therefore I tell you, whatever you ask for in prayer, believe that you have received it, and it will be yours."*
>
> —Mark 11:22–24 NIV

The danger of misusing scripture is always present. Some have used this verse to promote a selfish "name it and claim it" theology. Others misuse it as an invitation to demand God provide whatever our imperfect, short-sighted, and selfish will might desire. We must always interpret scripture to conform with God's "good, pleasing, and perfect will" and not impose our will upon God.

Another concern regarding this passage is that most of us have not succeeded in moving mountains into the sea because we believe. But conversely, I suspect most of us have created immovable mountains in our minds because of negative beliefs.

When we believe something is *not* possible for us to accomplish, it is not possible. At times, we create immovable mountains out of molehills with our negative faith or misbeliefs. When we speak limiting messages to ourselves, we hinder ourselves. Today's lesson is about finding the inhibitions in our mind—untrue beliefs that limit our effectiveness or growth. It's time to stop creating obstacles (mountains) in our minds and start moving them into the sea!

Jesus, you taught us to pray: "Thy Kingdom come, Thy will be done on earth as it is in heaven." But often, my misbeliefs hinder your will. Forgive me. Show me how to replace the inhibitions (negative beliefs) about myself with positive beliefs about you. Transform my life and set me free to be and to do all you desire for me. Amen.

Invincible

- Complete the Sherpa Training Session 6: Who Says You Can't?
- Video, 100 Exercise, and X Challenge

Involved

> *Do not conform to the pattern of this world, but be transformed by the renewing of your mind. Then you will be able to test and approve what God's will is—His good, pleasing and perfect will.*
>
> —Romans 12:2–3 NIV

The pattern of this world often limits us from living according to God's plans and purposes. We often feel the world prohibits us from walking in the footsteps of Christ Jesus. We experience this outside pressure as prohibition. Prohibitions restrict, limit, and communicate what you cannot do.

It's time to challenge prohibitions from the world and courageously stand for God's grace, mercy, justice, righteousness, and love, even if there may be consequences.

Let's discern how the world puts inhibitions into our heads that keep us from being Christlike. Inhibitions are internal limiting beliefs that hinder your ability to act. We often project those inhibitions outward and define them as prohibitions. We blame circumstances and others, thinking, *"They won't let me."* Enough! Instead of making excuses, let's work around, jump over, or fill in the gap and resolve the situation.

Whether you are struggling with prohibitions or inhibitions holding you back, ask God to reveal, transform, and renew the patterns of your mind.

Lord, I no longer want to live conforming to the pattern of this world. Transform my life by renewing my mind. Help me discern when prohibitions are helpful and when prohibitions are limiting my faith. I don't want either prohibitions or inhibitions to keep me from glorifying you and blessing others. Help me see when inhibitions keep me from being all you want me to be. I no longer want to blame others for holding me back. Fill me with your presence and empower me to walk with you. I want to do your good, pleasing, and perfect will in thought, attitude, speech, and action. Amen.

For Reflection or Discussion

1. When we believe something is *not* possible for us to accomplish, it is not possible. Can you think of a time in your life when this happened?
2. What inhibitions (negative beliefs or limiting messages) have become insurmountable mountains in

your mind? What would you need to believe to cast them into the sea?

3. What prohibitions feel like barriers, hurdles, and gaps holding you back?
4. What did you learn about the difference between barriers, hurdles, and gaps from this week's videos?
5. In what area does your mind want to say "they won't let me" when, in fact, there may be a way to work around, jump over, or fill the gap and move forward? What is the cost of your inhibition?
6. It's easier to blame others and define a lack of progress as a prohibition. When might you have blamed others instead of taking responsibility for the situation?
7. What thought patterns in your mind merit transforming?
8. Describe a beneficial prohibition, and then challenge one that is not helpful.
9. From what pattern of this world would you like to be transformed by the renewal of your mind?
10. Describe how inhibitions or prohibitions are keeping you from glorifying God and blessing others?

7

CORE Process

Invited

> *Be very careful, then, how you live—not as unwise but as wise, making the most of every opportunity, because the days are evil. Therefore do not be foolish, but understand what the Lord's will is.*
>
> —Ephesians 5:15–17 NIV

Every day we are presented with:

- Opportunities to learn and grow,
- Opportunities to gain self-awareness, and
- Opportunities to capture our insights and "marry self-awareness to action."

Unwise people overlook these opportunities. The wise make the most of them. Avoiding learning opportunities is foolish. Gaining understanding and obeying God's will is the Lord's desire for us.

Lord, help me become more self-aware as I go about my day. Show me the learning opportunities you put before me and guide me as I use the CORE Process to gain insight, develop plans, and take action. Amen.

Invincible

- Complete the Sherpa Training Session 7: CORE Process
- Video, 100 Exercise, and X Challenge

Involved

To some who were confident of their own righteousness and looked down on everyone else, Jesus told this parable: "Two men went up to the temple to pray, one a Pharisee and the other a tax collector. The Pharisee stood by himself and prayed: 'God, I thank you that I am not like other people—robbers, evildoers, adulterers—or even like this tax collector. I fast twice a week and give a tenth of all I get.'

"But the tax collector stood at a distance. He would not even look up to heaven, but beat his breast and said, 'God, have mercy on me, a sinner.'

"I tell you that this man, rather than the other, went home justified before God. For all those who exalt themselves will be humbled, and those who humble themselves will be exalted."

—Luke 18:9–14 NIV

Jesus declares no quality is more important for a leader than a humble spirit before God and others. No quality is more important for personal and Christian growth.

The prideful ask the question "What is my learning opportunity today?" and miss the point. They can see all kinds of things the people around them ought to learn, but their pride keeps them from admitting what they should learn.

It is the same when reviewing or implementing new content, such as the GiANT tools we covered in the past few weeks. The prideful are quick to say, "I've got this!" They often don't understand that exposure to new ideas without implementing them gains nothing.

A humble approach embraces the value of understanding and implementing new tools for life.

God, grant me a humble heart, open and eager to learn, grow, and change. And help me to be a humble servant-leader who calibrates support and challenge well in every relationship. Amen.

Invested

A. Please identify your vital insight from this session and write it in your *Breakthrough* Journal.

B. For reflection or discussion:

We have covered a lot of ground in the first six sessions.

- Hurdles and Gaps
- The 100x Leader, the Mountain, and Sherpa
- The Peace Index
- The 70:30 Principle
- The Support/Challenge Matrix
- 5 Circles of Influence: Intentional vs. Accidental

- Know Yourself to Lead Yourself
- Who Says You Can't? Inhibition vs. Prohibition
- Barriers

1. What adjustments would help you become a humble servant-leader?
2. Which two concepts would benefit your family? When and how will you implement these?
3. Which two concepts would benefit your work team? When and how will you implement these?
4. Share a time when you demonstrated marrying self-awareness to action.
5. What new self-awareness have you gained in the past few weeks, and what action will you take at this time?
6. What is your learning opportunity for this week?
7. What happened? Just state the facts.
8. Why did it happen? What was your role in it?
9. What is your action plan for dealing with it?
10. What is your deadline and accountability plan?

8

5 Voices: Discover Your Leadership Voice

Invited

> *As Jesus and his disciples were on their way, he came to a village where a woman named Martha opened her home to him. She had a sister called Mary, who sat at the Lord's feet listening to what he said. But Martha was distracted by all the preparations that had to be made. She came to him and asked, "Lord, don't you care that my sister has left me to do the work by myself? Tell her to help me!"*
>
> *"Martha, Martha," the Lord answered, "you are worried and upset about many things, but few things are needed—or indeed only one. Mary has chosen what is better, and it will not be taken away from her."*
>
> —Luke 10:38–42 NIV

According to the customs of the day, Martha was doing the "right" things. She was preparing the house and the food for her guests. We might think of Martha as using her Nurturer voice. She focused on the practical, the here and now, providing care and hospitality and putting others' needs ahead of her own.

On the other hand, Mary may have been utilizing her Creative tendencies by thinking outside the box and social norms. Usually, it would be the men listening to the teacher in this patriarchal society. But Mary chose not to focus on the house and the food. She was interested in Jesus's teaching about the future and the Kingdom of heaven. She ignored the social conventions protecting the status quo and embraced the idea that Jesus was going to make things incredibly better.

Neither woman's response was right nor wrong. Neither was good or bad. No one sinned. Two women lived out of different God-given ways of seeing the world. They were wired differently.

We are embarking on a journey of self-discovery, through which we will be discerning our own "voice order." There is no hierarchy. There is no right or wrong. But there is an opportunity to understand how you see the world and why other people may see things differently. These are the voices we will be studying:

- The Nurturer: Champion of People
- The Creative: Champion of Innovation
- The Guardian: Champion of Due Diligence
- The Connector: Champion of Relational Networks
- The Pioneer: Champion of Strategy

Enjoy the 5 Voices journey!

Lord, reveal how you designed me. Help me understand that others have different perspectives. This is not right or wrong, not good or bad. Different viewpoints provide tremendous value when we appreci-

ate the gift each voice brings. Help me set aside my insecurities or self-preservation and welcome new perspectives. Amen.

Invincible

- Complete the Sherpa Training Session 8: Discover Your Leadership Voice
- Video, 100 Exercise, and X Challenge

Involved

> *So Christ himself gave the apostles, the prophets, the evangelists, the pastors and teachers, to equip his people for works of service, so that the body of Christ may be built up until we all reach unity in the faith and in the knowledge of the Son of God and become mature, attaining to the whole measure of the fullness of Christ.*
>
> —Ephesians 4:11–13 NIV

Let's look at a *loose* connection between the 5 Voices and the fivefold ministry gifts. For example:

- People with apostles' tendencies will likely have Pioneer tendencies.
- People with prophets' tendencies will likely have Creative tendencies.
- People with evangelists' tendencies will likely have Connector tendencies.

- People with pastors' tendencies will likely have Nurturer tendencies.
- People with teachers' tendencies will likely have Guardian tendencies.

Please note these two lists are not equal; the tendencies merely overlap.

It's also helpful to acknowledge the broad spectrum of how people express these tendencies.

People may exhibit tendencies with selfishness and immaturity or present tendencies with selflessness, maturity, or wisdom. Depending on the person, the life experiences, or the context, their behavior will be somewhere along a continuum between good and bad, helpful and harmful, godly or sinful.

The 5 Voices have no hierarchy and of themselves are neither good nor bad. The impact on others depends on how these voices are lived out through your attitudes, words, and actions.

Discovering our voice order is never an excuse for poor or harmful behavior towards others. But what we learn about ourselves in these lessons can provide insights into the unique challenges of allowing the Holy Spirit to establish Christlikeness and the fruit of the Spirit in our lives.

Dear Lord, help me recognize how insights I gain this month from the 5 Voices can be part of your plan for my sanctification and Christian growth. Help me discover ways to use my unique Voice combination for your purposes. Amen.

Invested

A. Please identify your vital insight from this session and write it in your *Breakthrough* Journal.

B. For reflection or discussion:

1. Are you naturally more like Mary or Martha?
2. What are your top three Voices?
3. What self-awareness insights have you gained from these Voices?
4. What have you discovered about how others might be experiencing you?
5. Have you encouraged a family member or teammate to take the assessment? What have you learned about them from the 5 Voices?
6. Knowing your 5 Voices, how might you intentionally adjust your communication tendencies to get your message across effectively?
7. Knowing others are not like you, how might you adjust your listening skills to improve your understanding of others' perspectives and communication?
8. How might understanding the voices of your team help you become a better team leader?
9. How do you relate with the fivefold ministry gifts of apostle, prophet, evangelist, pastor, and teacher?
10. How might understanding your Voice order inform your faith journey and growth path to becoming more Christlike?

9

Leadership Insights for Your Voice

Invited

Peter is often our favorite of Jesus's disciples, perhaps because his strengths and flaws are readily apparent. Here is a quick list of some of Peter's failures.

- Peter looks away from Jesus and fails to "continue" to walk on water. (Matt. 14:22)
- Peter speaks in a holy moment on the Mount of Transfiguration and offers to build three shelters for Jesus, Moses, and Elijah. (Matt. 17:4 and Mark 9:5)
- Peter speaks for Jesus, without consulting Him, and commits Jesus to pay the two-drachma tax. (Matt. 17:24)
- Peter answers the question correctly, saying: "You are the Christ, the son of the living God." (Matt. 16:16)
- Peter resists the most significant reason Jesus became a human: the atonement for human sin. Jesus severely rebukes Peter: "Get behind me, Satan!" (Matt. 16:23)

- Peter resists when Jesus moves to wash Peter's feet. (John 13:8)
- Peter fails to stand by Jesus and falls asleep in the Garden of Gethsemane. (Matt. 16:23)
- Peter denies Jesus with "oaths" and "curses" in the public arena. (Matt. 26:74)
- Peter is overwhelmed by his sin, discovers his weakness, quits the Apostolic Team, and goes back to his comfortable roots: fishing. (John 21)

Peter displays many characteristics of an immature Connector voice: a magnetic personality, impulsivity, outspokenness, and expansive thinking. He might have benefited from understanding the leadership insights for his voice.

What is your primary voice? How might the leadership insights for that voice help you follow Christ and stay out of trouble?

Lord Jesus, I want to follow you and reflect your likeness. But the unchecked tendencies of my primary voice might hinder this possibility. Teach me to maximize my voice strengths and minimize weaknesses, so you bless others through me. Amen.

Invincible

- Complete the Sherpa Training Session 9: Leadership Insights
- Video, 100 Exercise, and X Challenge

Involved

Meanwhile, Saul was still breathing out murderous threats against the Lord's disciples. He went to the high priest and asked him for letters to the synagogues in Damascus, so that if he found any there who belonged to the Way, whether men or women, he might take them as prisoners to Jerusalem. As he neared Damascus on his journey, suddenly a light from heaven flashed around him. He fell to the ground and heard a voice say to him, "Saul, Saul, why do you persecute me?"

"Who are you, Lord?" Saul asked.

"I am Jesus, whom you are persecuting," he replied. Now get up and go into the city, and you will be told what you must do."

—Acts 9:1–6 NIV

Transforming the heart and mind of a strong Pioneer Voice does not happen immediately or easily. It took a flash of light, blindness, healing, and three years in the Arabian desert for God to transform Saul of Tarsus into Paul the Apostle.

Whatever your primary voice may be, changing to reflect Christlikeness is rarely immediate or easily accomplished.

Are you still waiting for a bolt of lightning to knock you off your horse? What will it take for you to repent of the things separating you from God's best for your life?

Lord Jesus, am I still waiting for some supernatural intervention to change my life on the road toward my Damascus? If so, I am not responsibly listening to your Word. Help me repent (turn around) when I am going the wrong way, and let me follow you. Forgive me. Help me. Teach me. Train me. Mold me. Use me. Amen.

Invested

A. Please identify your vital insight from this session and write it in your *Breakthrough* Journal.

B. For reflection or discussion:

We all have strengths and weaknesses. Each of the 5 Voices also has opportunities and pitfalls.

1. What strengths of your voice might Christ use?
2. What do you see as the weaknesses of your voice that the enemy will try to use?
3. How might the leadership insights of your primary voice help you follow Christ?
4. Each voice has its challenges. Identify someone in your sphere of influence who exhibits each voice and share how you might help them learn and grow toward Christlikeness. Use the following statements to guide your thinking.

    a. **Nurturers:** learn to bring effective challenges and provide accountability.

    b. **Creatives**: realize perfection can be a curse and good enough is often good enough.

    c. **Guardians**: release the need for control and begin taking appropriate risks.

    d. **Connectors**: stop being easily offended by taking feedback so personally.

    e. **Pioneers**: understand winning isn't everything.

10

5 Voices: Weapon Systems and Negative Impact

Invited

Therefore, just as sin entered the world through one man, and death through sin, and in this way death came to all people, because all sinned—

But the gift is not like the trespass. For if the many died by the trespass of the one man, how much more did God's grace and the gift that came by the grace of the one man, Jesus Christ, overflow to the many! Nor can the gift of God be compared with the result of one man's sin: The judgment followed one sin and brought condemnation, but the gift followed many trespasses and brought justification. For if, by the trespass of the one man, death reigned through that one man, how much more will those who receive God's abundant provision of grace and of the gift of righteousness reign in life through the one man, Jesus Christ!

—Romans 5:12, 15–17 NIV

God created humans in God's image. But sin entered and damaged everyone and everything. Therefore, we all need salvation through Jesus Christ. It sounds simple, but we live in a confusing time of "already and not yet." Christ already won the victory 2,000 years ago, and yet we live in a world overrun by sin and the devil. We await the victorious second coming of our Messiah and King.

What does this have to do with the 5 Voices? Each voice has a shadow side. Each voice uses a weapon of choice. Sin abounds, and there are power struggles between humans. Weapons are launched, and people are wounded. Yet, as Christ's people, we confront sin in ourselves and allow his power to make us overcomers.

Today's session revolves around these questions:

- What is my weapon of choice? Do I use more than one?
- When and why have I used these weapons? How have my weapons damaged others?
- How can I put down my weapons and pick up the righteousness of Christ?

The weapons most often used by the 5 Voices include:

- Pioneer: a shoulder-mounted grenade launcher
- Connector: information warfare—poisons the reputation of an enemy
- Guardian: the interrogation chamber

- Creatives fall into two camps:
  - Creative-Pioneer: sniper rifle (one armor-piercing piece of logic takes out a rival)
  - Creative-Connector: The Incredible Hulk (rage) takes over when values are violated
- Nurturer: first aid kit—they either "kill them with kindness" or punish by withdrawing care

Pay keen attention while watching the videos to understand which weapons you may have used.

Lord, help me see which weapons I may have used. Forgive me for damaging others with these weapons. Reveal the pathway of faith and righteousness. I no longer want to be a conduit of harm; let me be a conduit of Life through Christ! Amen.

Invincible

- Complete the Sherpa Training Session 10: Weapon Systems
- Video, 100 Exercise, and X Challenge

Involved

> *If we claim to be without sin, we deceive ourselves and the truth is not in us. If we confess our sins, he is faithful and just and will forgive us our sins and purify us from all unrighteousness. If we claim we have not sinned, we make him out to be a liar and his word is not in us.*

> *But if we walk in the light, as he is in the light, we have fellowship with one another, and the blood of Jesus, his Son, purifies us from all sin.*
>
> —1 John 1:8–10, 7 NIV

If we claim we have never used any of the 5 Voices' weapons, we may deceive ourselves. It is a rare individual who has never taken out one of these weapons and used it against others. Most of us realize we have used one or more of these weapons on numerous occasions.

This week's exercise reflects on our primary and secondary weapons. The first step is making a list of times we pulled out our weapons, including the places and people involved. Then consider who deserves an apology. Third, prayerfully set a time and place to meet with that person and make amends.

Lord Jesus, I trust God is faithful to forgive my sins and cleanse me from all unrighteousness. But people are not always so gracious. Help me walk in the light, make apologies where necessary, ask forgiveness, and restore fellowship where my weapons have caused problems. I trust the blood of Jesus purifies me from all sin. Let your love flow through my apologies to heal any hurts I have inflicted upon others. Amen.

Invested

A. Please identify your vital insight from this session and write it in your *Breakthrough* Journal.

B. For reflection or discussion:

1. When you look at the weapons of the 5 Voices, what weapon have you used?
2. What might be your secondary weapon? Do you use any others? In what settings or situations?
3. What weapon have you used in your family?
4. What weapon have you used in the church community?
5. What weapon have you used at work?
6. Who deserves an apology for the way you used your weapon against them?
7. When and where can you accomplish this?
8. How might you make amends to the recipients of your weaponry?
9. What are your memories of someone using these weapons against you?
10. What will it take for you to forgive that person and let go of the offense and the hurt?

11

5 Voices: What Triggers Your Weapon System?

Invited

> *We all stumble in many ways. Anyone who is never at fault in what they say is perfect, able to keep their whole body in check.*
>
> *When we put bits into the mouths of horses to make them obey us, we can turn the whole animal. Or take ships as an example. Although they are so large and are driven by strong winds, they are steered by a very small rudder wherever the pilot wants to go. Likewise, the tongue is a small part of the body, but it makes great boasts. Consider what a great forest is set on fire by a small spark.*
>
> —James 3:2–5 NIV

A small spark can start a great forest fire. It can be a situation, action, or comment from someone that creates a fire within us. Without grace and self-control, we will likely pull out our weapons and go on the attack. Knowing what triggers us is essential. Just as we can step on a small spark or flame to keep it from growing into a forest fire, we can learn to quench the power of a trigger so we don't overreact.

When we learn the kinds of things that may trigger the voice-weapon of our spouse, boss, or coworker, we can avoid setting them off. Limiting the use of weapons creates greater peace and productivity on many levels.

Lord, I don't ever want to make mountains out of molehills. I don't want to pull out heavy artillery because something triggers me. I don't want to see forest fires raging because of a small spark. Help me use this lesson on triggers to bring greater peace and productivity to my life, family, and workplace. Amen.

Invincible

- Complete the Sherpa Training Session 11: Triggers
- Video, 100 Exercise, and X Challenge

Involved

Interrogation can be designed to entrap! Three groups sought to ensnare Jesus, and each asked him a tough question they thought would bring him down. But his answers left them speechless and astonished. Then Jesus posed a question of his own (Matt. 22:15–46).

- The Herodians asked a political question: v. 15–17.
- The Sadducees asked a doctrinal question: v. 23–28.

- The Pharisees asked an ethical question: v. 34–36.
- Then Jesus asked a personal question that turned the tables on them: v. 41–45.

Let's use the first question about paying Caesar's imperial tax as our prime example.

> *Then the Pharisees went out and laid plans to trap him in his words. They sent their disciples to him along with the Herodians. "Teacher," they said, "we know that you are a man of integrity and that you teach the way of God in accordance with the truth. You aren't swayed by others, because you pay no attention to who they are. Tell us then, what is your opinion? Is it right to pay the imperial tax to Caesar or not?"*
>
> *But Jesus, knowing their evil intent, said, "You hypocrites, why are you trying to trap me? Show me the coin used for paying the tax." They brought him a denarius, and he asked them, "Whose image is this? And whose inscription?"*
>
> *"Caesar's," they replied.*
>
> *Then He said to them, "So give back to Caesar what is Caesar's, and to God what is God's."*
>
> *When they heard this, they were amazed. So they left him and went away.*
>
> —Matthew 22:15–22 NIV

Jesus, operating in the wisdom and power of God, knew how to deflect the questions meant to entrap him. He used the situation as a teaching moment for the listeners (including us!). Jesus didn't take the bait and let the attack trigger his weapon system. He didn't lose his cool, and he didn't play the victim. Unfortunately, most of us can remember times when we felt like a victim of a guardian's interrogation weapon.

Questions can intimidate, throw others off balance, or entrap. The Guardian's weapon, Interrogation, uses questions in this way. The Herodians, Sadducees, and Pharisees would have seen themselves as the good guys in their story—those who guarded the faith and protected the people from heresy. We see in this passage how they used interrogation questions in an attempt to make their case.

We have all seen examples in movies and television of interrogation being used to obtain information or the "truth." Yet, there are times when the length and severity of the interrogation make an innocent person lie and admit committing a crime they did not commit simply to make the interrogation stop.

The Guardian voice questions others in a desire to discover the reality or truth of a situation. This investigation can be a necessary and valuable contribution the Guardian's voice offers the group. But when Guardians interrogate as a weapon, they may leave people damaged or in pain.

Dear Lord, please teach me how to respond with the wisdom of Jesus instead of attacking or playing the victim when another person draws their weapon against me. Reveal what triggers me and how I can avoid the trap of reacting and losing my cool. I want to influence others (lead) without pulling out my weapon and damaging anyone. Please help me respond to others rather than react. Help me act intentionally rather than attack. Help me be more like you! Amen.

Invested

A. Please identify your vital insight from this session and write it in your *Breakthrough* Journal.

B. For reflection or discussion:

Look at the *Triggers* chart and answer the following:

1. What are the triggers of your top voices that can set you on edge?
2. What do these triggers reveal about your values, and what motivates you?
3. What attitude, way of speaking, habit, or trait do you exhibit that might trigger a Nurturer?
4. What attitude, way of speaking, habit, or trait do you exhibit that might trigger a Creative/Pioneer?
5. What attitude, way of speaking, habit, or trait do you exhibit that might trigger a Creative/Connector?
6. What attitude, way of speaking, habit, or trait do you exhibit that might trigger a Guardian?
7. What attitude, way of speaking, habit, or trait do you exhibit that might trigger a Connector?
8. What attitude, way of speaking, habit, or trait do you exhibit that might trigger a Pioneer?
9. How do you respond when someone uses these weapons on you?
10. What does Christ want you to do with your weapon? How does Christ want you to respond when another uses their weapon on you?

12

5 Voices: Rules of Engagement

Invited

> *Therefore, as God's chosen people, holy and dearly loved, clothe yourselves with compassion, kindness, humility, gentleness and patience.*
>
> —Colossians 3:12 NIV

Too many leaders believe success comes from dominating their followers. There is a better way. Servant leadership uses a different mindset, realizing that authentic influence combines strength and humility. Jesus models compassion and respect for others, not domination.

Strong voices with strong personalities often have a difficult time believing their followers also have good ideas. People in leadership who imagine they possess greater understanding than anyone else will miss opportunities to use their team's expertise.

The best leaders surround themselves with people who are experts in areas in which the leader does not have expertise. Listening to wise council provides valuable information for planning and decision-making.

Using the "softer to louder" voice order in meetings not only honors the contribution each person brings to the table but also delivers the best decision-making. What is this talking order?

- First: Nurturer voices
- Second: Creative voices
- Third: Guardian voices
- Fourth: Connector voices
- Fifth: Pioneer voices

Leaders with louder voices, you would be wise to:

- Take off your arrogant blinders ("I'm the only one who can see anything").
- Listen to everyone else's view first.
- Gain the best insights from every viewpoint.
- Incorporate them into your thinking.

God has not created various people who bring different perspectives simply to have strong (loud voices) dominate the weak (softer voices). An accurate understanding of a complicated situation may only be reached by gleaning multiple perspectives. Only when leaders "clothe" themselves in compassion, kindness, and gentleness will the team have the freedom to speak the truth from their perspective. Only when leaders "clothe" themselves with humility and patience will they hear what they can only learn from their team's diverse voices.

Lord, one thing I know is I don't know it all! Help me value the insights of those you have put around me who have different perspectives. Help me learn from people who are not like me. Help me appreciate what each of the 5 Voices brings to the table. Let me honor God by treating the people on my team well. Amen.

Invincible

- Complete the Sherpa Training Session 12: Rules of Engagement
- Video, 100 Exercise, and X Challenge

Involved

> *It was just before the Passover Festival. Jesus knew that the hour had come for him to leave this world and go to the Father. Having loved his own who were in the world, he loved them to the end…*
>
> *Jesus knew that the Father had put all things under his power, and that he had come from God and was returning to God; so he got up from the meal, took off his outer clothing, and wrapped a towel around his waist. After that, he poured water into a basin and began to wash his disciples' feet, drying them with the towel that was wrapped around him…*
>
> *Now that I, your Lord and Teacher, have washed your feet, you also should wash one another's feet. I have set you an example that you should do as I have done for you.*
>
> —John 13:1, 3–5, 14–15 NIV

Here Jesus demonstrates authentic servant leadership. In his world, a household servant would have washed the feet of those coming in from walking dirt streets in sandals. Jesus humbled himself and took on the role of a servant.

Our world is different. No servant ever washed my feet when I entered a friend's house. Our streets are paved, and I usually wear shoes and socks. So how can we model the servant leadership of Jesus in today's workplace? By making sure we value and hear all the voices around the table.

Drawing out the best of each person's voice and utilizing their strengths values them and their contributions. When a leader is humble and incorporates others' contributions into the decision-making process, the team and company benefit from improved outcomes.

When a leader considers the "softer voices" first and uses engagement rules, the team feels honored and appreciated. They usually respond by bringing their best efforts.

Think of Jesus washing the disciples' feet when you practice the rules of engagement with your team. Let humility and respect for those on your team empower everyone to collaborate for more significant achievements.

Jesus, you shocked your team when you washed their feet, then you told them to do as you had done for them. Help me humbly treat my team with dignity, value each person, and draw out the best in them by practicing the communication order and engagement rules I learned today. Let this be my way of following your example and washing the feet of others. Amen.

Invested

A. Please identify your vital insight from this session and write it in your *Breakthrough* Journal.

B. For reflection or discussion:

Look at the *Rules of Engagement* chart and answer the following:

1. What have you learned about yourself when you see the 5 Voices Rules of Engagement?
2. Name a Nurturer in your world and what you have learned about engaging with them.
3. Name a Creative in your world and what you have learned about engaging with them.
4. Name a Guardian in your world and what you have learned about engaging with them.
5. Name a Connector in your world and what you have learned about engaging with them.
6. Name a Pioneer in your world and what you have learned about engaging with them.
7. What are your thoughts about the term *servant leadership*?
8. What examples of people that have demonstrated servant leadership can you name?
9. What made their leadership effective?
10. Why did Jesus wash his disciples' feet? How might you "wash the feet" of those you lead?

13

5 Voices Liberation Statements

Invited

Just as a body, though one, has many parts, but all its many parts form one body, so it is with Christ....

Even so the body is not made up of one part but of many.

Now if the foot should say, "Because I am not a hand, I do not belong to the body," it would not for that reason stop being part of the body. And if the ear should say, "Because I am not an eye, I do not belong to the body," it would not for that reason stop being part of the body. If the whole body were an eye, where would the sense of hearing be? If the whole body were an ear, where would the sense of smell be? But in fact God has placed the parts in the body, every one of them, just as He wanted them to be. If they were all one part, where would the body be? As it is, there are many parts, but one body....

...there should be no division in the body, but that its parts should have equal concern for each other. If one part suffers, every part suffers with it; if one part is honored, every part rejoices with it.

—1 Corinthians 12:12, 14–20, 25–26 NIV

Birds of a feather do *flock together*, and similar voices often appreciate each other. Pioneers enjoy sharing how they will "take over the world." Connectors enjoy discussing how they will create collaboration to bring about a significant improvement. Creatives may be thinking years ahead of anyone else, either pointing at future possibilities or dangers around the corner that others cannot see. Guardians enjoy others who understand the value of doing "due diligence" and getting the details right. Nurturers gather to meet the needs of people.

But if you are working with a team of 10 people, they are not likely to be of all one voice. A team will be stronger if all 5 Voices are present. Which highlights the danger of "disregarding those who don't think like me."

Paul compares the diversity in a group with the variety of limbs and organs in the human body. Let us apply this biblical truth to our teams and value the contribution of each member. We need each other, and we should have "equal concern for each other." We are in this together.

So let's learn from today's Liberation Statements how each of the 5 Voices can help people play their God-given roles to the best of their abilities. Let us help those around us (especially those who are unlike us) become all God wants them to be.

Lord, forgive me for wishing everyone were like me (as if I am so great). Help me build a team that understands and values each person's voice and releases the contribution each brings for the good of the whole. Help us see we are better because of diversity. Help the parts of our team honor and care for one another. Amen.

Invincible

- Complete the Sherpa Training Session 13: Liberation Statements
- Video, 100 Exercise, and X Challenge

Involved

> *[Jesus] went to Nazareth, where he had been brought up, and on the Sabbath day he went into the synagogue, as was his custom. He stood up to read, and the scroll of the prophet Isaiah was handed to him. Unrolling it, he found the place where it is written:*
>
> *"The Spirit of the Lord is on me, because he has anointed me to proclaim good news to the poor. He has sent me to proclaim freedom for the prisoners and recovery of sight for the blind, to set the oppressed free, to proclaim the year of the Lord's favor."*
>
> *Then he rolled up the scroll, gave it back to the attendant and sat down. The eyes of everyone in the synagogue were fastened on him. He began by saying to them, "Today this scripture is fulfilled in your hearing."*
>
> —Luke 4:16–21 NIV

In 2018, the company oGoLead fielded national research and found evidence of massive feelings of lack of recognition in the workplace: "82 percent of employees feel their supervisor doesn't recognize them for what they do." You might say that in the workplace, the vast majority of people feel voiceless and unnoticed as if they are working for supervisors who don't understand or recognize their contribution.

Validating the 5 Voices around your conference table may seem like nothing compared to Jesus's mission to set the oppressed free. But don't underestimate the life-transforming power released for your team when you learn how to liberate each foundational voice. It's amazing what happens when you value people's voices and set them free to become all God created them to be!

Jesus, let me join your work of setting the oppressed free and proclaiming the Lord's favor. Use the concept of Liberating the 5 Voices in my team to help us contribute fully and be fully appreciated. Thank you that liberating others will make my team more efficient, effective, productive, and profitable! Amen.

Invested

A. Please identify your vital insight from this session and write it in your *Breakthrough* Journal.

B. For reflection or discussion:

Look at the *Liberation Statements* chart and answer the following:

1. What do you enjoy about gathering with people who share your voice?
2. Which voices are more challenging for you to be around?
3. Name a Nurturer in your world and describe how you can help liberate them.
4. Name a Creative in your world and describe how you can help liberate them.
5. Name a Guardian in your world and describe how you can help liberate them.
6. Name a Connector in your world and describe how you can help liberate them.
7. Name a Pioneer in your world and describe how you can help liberate them.

8. Imagine the life-transforming power of liberating each foundational voice in your family or team. Share a description of what you imagine.
9. How might you proclaim the Lord's favor to each of your family or team members?
10. Make a plan for increasing affirmation and appreciation of your family or team members' unique voices. Share your plan with the group.

14

5 Voices: CORE Process Game Plan

Invited

I praise you because I am fearfully and wonderfully made; your works are wonderful, I know that full well.

—Psalm 139:14 NIV

As we discover our Voice order, coming to peace and accepting how we are wired is very important. We are tempted to think, "I wish I were more like that," or perhaps, "My life would be so much better if I operated from that Voice." Embracing this thought is like saying, "I wish I were seven feet tall so I could play in the NBA." You can wish all you want, but it doesn't change the fact that you are five-foot-nine. Also, wishing may block you from embracing the valuable gifts and unique contribution God created you to make.

Can you accept and believe you are fearfully and wonderfully made and God has a unique purpose for your life? No one else on earth duplicates your mind, body, experiences, and relationships.

As we continue learning about ourselves, our Voice order, and our tendencies, don't push God out of the picture. Invite

God to reveal the wonder of who you are and the value you have as one of God's wonderful works.

> *Search me, God, and know my heart; test me and know my anxious thoughts. See if there is any offensive way in me, and lead me in the way everlasting.*
>
> —Psalm 139:23–24 NIV

Psalm 139 ends with the Psalmist essentially saying, "What is my learning opportunity?" It is another way of saying, "Where have I gone wrong? What requires change? Where is the path to a better me?"

As you use the CORE process to Know Yourself and Lead Yourself by focusing on Learning Opportunities for self, family, and team, let these verses from Psalm 139 inform your thinking. Let's offer them as a prayer:

Lord, I praise you because I am fearfully and wonderfully made; your works are wonderful; I know that full well. Search me, God, and know my heart; test me and know my anxious thoughts. See if there is any offensive way in me and lead me in the way everlasting. Amen.

Invincible

- Complete the Sherpa Training Session 14: CORE Process for 5 Voices
- Video, 100 Exercise, and X Challenge

Involved

> *For the kingdom of heaven is like a man traveling to a far country, who called his own servants and delivered his goods to them. And to one he gave five talents, to another two, and to another one, to each according to his own*

ability; and immediately he went on a journey. Then he who had received the five talents went and traded with them, and made another five talents. And likewise he who had received two gained two more also. But he who had received one went and dug in the ground, and hid his lord's money. After a long time the lord of those servants came and settled accounts with them.

So he who had received five talents came and brought five other talents, saying, "Lord, you delivered to me five talents; look, I have gained five more talents besides them." His lord said to him, "Well done, good and faithful servant; you were faithful over a few things, I will make you ruler over many things. Enter into the joy of your lord." He also who had received two talents came and said, "Lord, you delivered to me two talents; look, I have gained two more talents besides them." His lord said to him, "Well done, good and faithful servant; you have been faithful over a few things, I will make you ruler over many things. Enter into the joy of your lord."

Then he who had received the one talent came and said, "Lord, I knew you to be a hard man, reaping where you have not sown, and gathering where you have not scattered seed. And I was afraid, and went and hid your talent in the ground. Look, there you have what is yours."

But his lord answered and said to him, "You wicked and lazy servant, you knew that I reap where I have not sown, and gather where I have not scattered seed. So you ought to have deposited my money with the bankers, and at my coming I would have received back my own with interest. So take the talent from him, and give it to him who has ten talents.

"For to everyone who has, more will be given, and he will have abundance; but from him who does not have, even what he has will be taken away."

—Matthew 25:14–29 NKJV

Think about your combination of the 5 Voices as the "talents" the Master bestowed upon you. Don't get caught wondering whether you were given one, or two, or five talents—that is a trap. Rejoice in the talents you have been given, and *choose* to invest them well.

- Learn as much as you can about your talents (Voices and Voice order).
- Use the power of your voice with wisdom, maturity, and compassion.
- Maximize the gifts of your primary Voice.
- Mitigate (or eliminate) the unnecessary use of your Voice weapons.
- Become conscious of how triggers might set you off and how to avoid falling into old habits.
- Use the rules of engagement and liberation statements to bring out the best in others.
- *Invest* your talents (God-given Voice) for God's glory and honor. Multiply their value by utilizing them to bless others and improve relationships, systems, and productivity. Let your talents (Voice tendencies) create a profit for your loving Master who created you!

Lord Jesus, you have wired my life to perceive and think and respond and act in unique ways. Let me invest this gift (talents) of my Voice tendencies for the blessing of others and the glory of God. Amen.

Invested

A. Please identify your vital insight from this session and write it in your *Breakthrough* Journal.

B. For reflection or discussion:

We have covered the Voices, Voice order, Leadership Insights, Weapons, Triggers, Rules for engagement, and Liberation statements.

1. What valuable insights about yourself have you gained?
2. Which insights about family or team have been most helpful?
3. How has self-awareness increased?
4. What steps will help you "marry self-awareness to action"?
5. If you could have another of the 5 Voices, which one would you choose? Why?
6. Since you are "fearfully and wonderfully made" by God, how might you better accept and celebrate the distinct voice you have?
7. How might your unique voice be a part of God's distinctive plan and purpose for your life?
8. How might you invest your talents (God-given Voice) for God's glory and honor?

9. How might your unique talents (voice) be multiplied in value by utilizing them to bless others and improve relationships, systems, and productivity?
10. How might your talents (Voice tendencies) create a profit for your loving Master who created you?

15

5 Gears: The Core of Your Leadership

Invited

> *Be on your guard; stand firm in the faith; be courageous; be strong. Do everything in love.*
>
> —1 Corinthians 16:13–14 NIV

It takes courage to look at ourselves and be honest about what we see. The depth of courage, insight, and honesty you use for today's lesson will determine the value of what you discover. The greater the depth, the higher the reward. Go for it!

And at the same time, be kind. Use *blameless discernment*. As you assess yourself, *"Do everything in love."*

Today we assess three aspects of ourselves.

1. IQ: Competency (Knowledge and Skills)
2. EQ: Connectivity (Emotional Intelligence)
3. PQ: Self-Awareness (Personality Quotient)

The relative size of each circle reflects your development in that area. The circles don't have to be equal, but if one is significantly underdeveloped, that area needs attention. Let the Holy Spirit guide your self-assessment and give you insights into God's plan for your growth.

The area where all three circles overlap is called the Core. In the human body, core exercises are those using your midsection without support, like push-ups, sit-ups, and abdominal crunches. These exercises strengthen and train your lower back, hips, and abdomen to work together for better balance and stability.

With a stronger inner-core, your whole life will have better balance and stability and greater fulfillment and success! Strengthen the inner-core by growing all your circles, with special efforts to expand your smallest circle, whether IQ, EQ, or PQ.

Lord, please give me the courage and compassion to assess myself well. Then grant me the strength to grow and develop my core. Amen.

Invincible

- Complete the Sherpa Training Session 15: The Core of Your Leadership
- Video, 100 Exercise, and X Challenge

Involved

Good people, cheer GOD! *Right-living people sound best when praising.*
Use guitars to reinforce your Hallelujahs! Play his praise on a grand piano!
Invent your own new song to him; give him a trumpet fanfare.
For **GOD's Word is solid to the core**; *everything he makes is sound inside and out.*
He loves it when everything fits, when his world is in plumb-line true.
Earth is drenched in GOD*'s affectionate satisfaction.*

—Psalm 33:1–5 MSG, (emphasis added)

This passage begins with praise, which is always a great place to start. Consider making a *cross of praise* every day.

- The vertical bar – reaching upward: Praise God for your gifts, talents, strengths! Bless the Lord for all you have received from God's bountiful hand.
- The horizontal bar – reaching outward: Praise others when they do well. Build people up with sincere appreciation.

Also, work at becoming *solid to the core* by putting on love, joy, peace, patience, kindness, goodness, faithfulness, and self-control.

Ask God to empower your growth in the areas of Competency, Connectivity, and Self-Awareness. Then let God direct the strength-building actions that can make you *solid to the core!*

Lord God, expand my smaller circle and strengthen me to become solid to the core. You love it when everything in my life fits. You delight when we are plumb-line true to your grace and mercy. Let our lives be drenched in your affectionate satisfaction! Amen.

Invested

A. Please identify your vital insight from this session and write it in your *Breakthrough* Journal.

B. For reflection or discussion:

1. What would change if you were to *do everything in love*? What would change in your self-understanding, your relationships, and your work?
2. How might your relationships at home and work be impacted if you considered them as praise to God?
3. *God's word is solid to the core*. What could put God's word at the core of your life?

Answer the following three questions (IQ, EQ, PQ) on a scale of 1–100:

4. How would you rate your competency, knowledge, and skills (IQ)? Why?
5. How would you rate your connectivity, relational abilities, and communication competence? (EQ) Why?
6. How well do you know yourself and your tendencies (PQ)? Why did you pick that number?
7. What are some strengths you can multiply by coaching others? What might a plan for their growth include?
8. What is an area of weakness in which you may grow? What would be some possible ways to increase your smallest circle?
9. What might an effective action plan for your growth include? How might your growth in this area give glory to God?

16

5 Gears: Over-Productive and Under-Present

Invited

Someone in the crowd said to him, "Teacher, tell my brother to divide the inheritance with me."

Jesus replied, "Man, who appointed me a judge or an arbiter between you?" Then he said to them, "Watch out! Be on your guard against all kinds of greed; life does not consist in an abundance of possessions."

And he told them this parable: "The ground of a certain rich man yielded an abundant harvest. He thought to himself, 'What shall I do? I have no place to store my crops.'

"Then he said, 'This is what I'll do. I will tear down my barns and build bigger ones, and there I will store my surplus grain. And I'll say to myself, "You have plenty of grain laid up for many years. Take life easy; eat, drink and be merry."'

"But God said to him, 'You fool! This very night your life will be demanded from you. Then who will get what you have prepared for yourself?'

"This is how it will be with whoever stores up things for themselves but is not rich toward God."

—Luke 12: 13–21 NIV

Being over-productive and under-present is a great danger in our individualized, competitive, and success-oriented society. The motto seems to be, "If you want to get ahead, you have to put in the overtime!"

It's not wrong to work hard or seek success, but too often this pursuit results in a person's failure as a spouse or parent. We have seen whole generations grow up with an absent parent figure, even when the marriages remain intact. It's tough to put in an overtime day and still have the energy to care for your family.

So we ask, "Isn't there a better way?" The 5 Gears can help with the idea of *time* management. Perhaps more importantly, the 5 Gears can help with the concept of *energy* management. Ultimately, the 5 Gears can help you learn to be more *present and productive* in both work and relationship settings.

People on their death bed rarely look back and wish they spent more time at the office. But all too often, people regret they didn't invest more in their marriage, children, and other significant relationships.

Ask yourself:

- Lord, where have I sold out and been shortsighted concerning my time and energy?
- Have I followed the societal herd chasing after material goods instead of seeking righteousness?

- How would you have me invest (or even give away) some of my time, which is one of my most valuable resources?
- How might I live a balanced and moderate life, free from building unnecessary and unhelpful barns to store more stuff?

Lord, productivity is good. You call us to live productive lives. But the enemy is continually trying to take good things and twist, distort, or blow them out of proportion until they become dangerous and damaging. Guard me against the hyper-productivity that could damage those I love. Show me how these 5 Gears help me become more present and productive. Amen.

Invincible

- Complete the Sherpa Training Session 16: Over-Productive and Under-Present
- Video, 100 Exercise, and X Challenge

Involved

> *Do not lay up for yourselves treasures on earth, where moth and rust destroy and where thieves break in and steal, but lay up for yourselves treasures in heaven, where neither moth nor rust destroys and where thieves do not break in and steal. For where your treasure is, there your heart will be also.*
>
> —Matthew 6:19–21 ESV

What do you treasure? Be careful what you treasure, for your heart will become invested there also.

I have friends whose daughter and son-in-law served as career missionaries to India for most of two decades. My friends discovered that with their treasure (children and grandchildren) in India, that is where their heart was also. Their thoughts, prayers, and finances focused on India. They would travel to India and enjoy their treasures (family) while helping in the mission's work whenever they could.

To paraphrase an old saying: *Use things and treasure people; don't treasure things and use people.*

Lord, help me live in such a way that I store up treasure in heaven. Show me how to be fully present and productive when I am at work and *shift gears and be fully present when I am at home. Help me give my best to those people I treasure. Teach me how to use the 5 Gears to demonstrate love for my family and friends. Amen.*

Invested

A. Please identify your vital insight from this session and write it in your *Breakthrough* Journal.

B. For reflection or discussion:

1. Who might accuse you of being over-productive and under-present? What is their evidence? How might they be right?
2. Where have you sold out to greed or the pursuit of success and been shortsighted concerning your time and energy?
3. When have you followed the societal herd chasing after material goods instead of seeking righteousness?

4. How would God have you invest (or even give away) some of your time, which is one of your most valuable resources?
5. How might you live a balanced and moderate life, free from building unnecessary and unhelpful barns to store more stuff?
6. What do you treasure? How is your heart invested there?
7. When are you in danger of using people and treasuring things? What changes might demonstrate that you use things and treasure people?
8. What would help you be more present and productive?
9. In what ways might you "trade up" and invest your time, energy, and activities?
10. What are some time wasters God may be calling you to give up?

17

5 Gears: Tool and Execution

Invited

For everything there is a season,
a time for every activity under heaven.
A time to be born and a time to die.
A time to plant and a time to harvest.
A time to kill and a time to heal.
A time to tear down and a time to build up.
A time to cry and a time to laugh.
A time to grieve and a time to dance.
A time to scatter stones and a time to gather stones.
A time to embrace and a time to turn away.
A time to search and a time to quit searching.
A time to keep and a time to throw away.
A time to tear and a time to mend.
A time to be quiet and a time to speak.
A time to love and a time to hate.
A time for war and a time for peace.

—Ecclesiastes 3:1–8 NLT

There is a time for each of the 5 Gears:

- A time for self-care and to *recharge* your batteries;
- A time to *connect* deeply with a family member, friend, or significant other;
- A time to be *social* with a group of people, interacting and being human together;
- A time to juggle multiple *tasks* and people, realizing the interruption *is* your work;
- A time to shut out the world and all distractions and *focus* on a project; and
- A time to apologize and be *responsive* to the reality your imperfections caused difficulty for another.

Get good at telling time and understanding what gear is necessary at a given time. Every one of us has one or two gears we naturally like and overuse. We also have one or two unnatural gears that we dislike and avoid.

Using each of the 5 Gears at the right time and place will foster success in relationships, business, and ministry. *There is a time for every activity under heaven.*

Author of time, guide my understanding of when, where, how, and with whom to use these gears. Forgive me for when my use of the wrong gear has caused difficulties for others. Help me forgive myself when I use unhelpful gears. Inspire me to use this simple concept in ways that will make profound changes in my life and enhance the lives of those I touch. Amen.

Invincible

- Complete the Sherpa Training Session 17: 5 Gears Tool
- Video, 100 Exercise, and X Challenge

Involved

The Lord *is the everlasting God, the Creator of the ends*
of the earth.
He will not grow tired or weary, and his understanding
no one can fathom.
He gives strength to the weary and increases the power of
the weak.
Even youths grow tired and weary, and young men
stumble and fall;
but those who hope in the Lord *will renew their*
strength.
They will soar on wings like eagles; they will run and not
grow weary,
they will walk and not be faint.

—Isaiah 40:28b–31 NIV

I learned to drive in a 1967 Opel Kadett with a four-on-the-floor stick shift. The underpowered vehicle would lurch, or the engine would die if you were in the wrong gear. I quickly learned how necessary it is to be in the right gear.

Mechanical engines run best at an optimal RPM, and so do our "human engines." If you are racing your engine too fast for too long, burnout is inevitable. If you don't use first and second gears appropriately, your engine will stall.

Many people don't realize how difficult they are making their own lives because they are not using the right gear at the right time. We often have moments when we feel weak, weary, tired, or faint because we are running in the wrong gear.

Every gear has a purpose and a place. When we use each of the 5 Gears at the right time, we renew our strength. We will keep our engine running smoothly and thus be able to "soar on wings like eagles... run and not grow weary... walk and not faint."

Lord, help me use the 5 Gears to maximize my day, time, energy, and resources. Help me gain comfort and skill with the gears that may be less natural to me. I realize all five are vital to living a productive and relationally present life. Help me become healthy and effective in each gear. Amen.

Invested

A. Please identify your vital insight from this session and write it in your *Breakthrough* Journal.

B. For reflection or discussion:

1. Which gear are you in the most?
2. Shifting into which gear is most challenging for you?
3. What is your action plan for improving your Gear health?
4. How might the 5 Gears help you maximize your time, resources, actions, and energy?
5. Where do your Gear tendencies match or contrast with those of your spouse or significant other?

6. How might this understanding (and some adjusting) strengthen your relationship?
7. Share a time (or pattern) when your use of the wrong gear has caused frustration for someone else.
8. How are your gear patterns making life more difficult for you? For those around you?
9. How might an adjustment on your part glorify God?
10. How might an adjustment on your part be a bless others?

18

5 Gears: Learning to Shift

Invited

> *I will give them an undivided heart and put a new spirit in them; I will remove from them their heart of stone and give them a heart of flesh. Then they will follow my decrees and be careful to keep my laws. They will be my people, and I will be their God.*
>
> —Ezekiel 11:19–20 NIV

People will experience you as "for them" when you choose the best gear for the situation. When you are in the wrong gear, people think you don't care. Learning to bring your focused attention is essential to connect and perform well.

In Second Gear, we practice connecting with an *undivided heart*. On many occasions, the mind and body are in different places. You might be at work and wishing you were at home. You might be at home and desiring to be out exercising. You might be out exercising and feel burdened and guilty you're not accomplishing work. Practice bringing your undivided heart to the person and the activity of the moment. Otherwise, you are wasting precious time, energy, and relational capital.

Lord, sometimes it seems I have a heart of pebbles—cold and hard as stone but divided into small pieces for all of the many things that are part of my world. Please give me an undivided heart. Enliven me with your spirit. Give me a heart of flesh that will be empathetic, compassionate, kind, and loving toward others. I surrender myself to you and trust you. Empower me to learn, grow, and develop as a person, a spouse/parent, a worker, a leader, and a follower of Christ. Amen.

Invincible

- Complete the Sherpa Training Session 18: Learning to Shift
- Video, 100 Exercise, and X Challenge

Involved

When the whole nation had finished crossing the Jordan, the LORD said to Joshua, "Choose twelve men from among the people, one from each tribe, and tell them to take up twelve stones from the middle of the Jordan, from right where the priests are standing, and carry them over with you and put them down at the place where you stay tonight."

So Joshua called together the twelve men he had appointed from the Israelites, one from each tribe, and said to them, "Go over before the ark of the LORD your God into the middle of the Jordan. Each of you is to take up a stone on his shoulder, according to the number of the tribes of the Israelites, to serve as a sign among you. In the future, when your children ask you, 'What do these stones mean?' tell them that the flow of the Jordan was cut off before the ark of the covenant of the LORD. When it crossed the Jordan, the waters of the Jordan were cut

> *off. These stones are to be a memorial to the people of Israel forever.*
>
> —Joshua 4:4–7 NIV

God instructed Israelites to establish a marker many times throughout the Scriptures. Markers served as a memorial, reminding them what God had done. Markers could serve as a useful prompt in our fast-paced society.

- What markers will help you remember to shift gears?
- What might help you get into the right gear at the right time to be more present and productive?
- What could help you learn how to be "for others" and give them your full and undivided attention when appropriate?
- What gear transitions might help reduce your tension, stress, and conflict?

Lord, please cause my PQ circle of self-awareness to grow so I can "know myself to lead myself" on a whole new level. Show me how to use the principle of the 5 Gears to improve my relationships and performance. Help these concepts stick in my mind and empower my actions. Thank you, Lord.

Invested

A. Please identify your vital insight from this session and write it in your *Breakthrough* Journal.

B. For reflection or discussion:

1. What would focusing your full and undivided attention mean to your spouse or child? What keeps you from giving them this gift?
2. What will you do to practice bringing your *undivided heart* (second gear) to a person you love?
3. How well do you use third gear small talk for connecting with people at work?
4. How well do you make transitions from third gear to fourth or fifth with your team?
5. How can these gears help you bring your best to each project or relationship?
6. What *markers* will help you remember to shift gears?
7. What might help you get into the right gear at the right time to be more present and productive?
8. What could help you learn how to be "for others" at work and give them your full and undivided attention when appropriate?
9. What gear transitions might help reduce your tension, anxiety, and conflict?
10. How might using these gears well help you demonstrate a "heart of flesh" that will be empathetic, compassionate, kind, and loving toward others?

19

CORE Process: Your 5 Gears Action Plan

Invited

> *But someone may say, "You have faith, and I have actions." Show me your faith without any actions, and I will show you my faith by my actions.*
>
> —James 2:18 ISV

Every gear can be overused or underused. People want to see whether we avoid extremes and live a full, balanced, productive life. What do your actions tell them?

Here are some examples of the overuse and underuse of these gears.

Fifth Gear – Focus

- Overuse: damaging others by shutting out coworkers, family, and friends in order to create or produce.

- Underuse: not revealing your best self (intelligence, ideas, productivity) because you lack the regular uninterruptable blocks of 45–90 minutes necessary to focus on creativity and productivity.

Fourth Gear – Tasks

- Overuse: juggling multiple tasks, seemingly 24/7, and continually being interrupted by the phone, email, texts, etc. Juggling tasks takes over your life and crowds out meaningful work (fifth), people time (second and third), or self-care (first).
- Underuse: stuck with the idea you cannot entertain a concept other than the one thing you have on your mind at this time.

Third Gear – Social

- Overuse: always on the run with people. Party, party, party!
- Underuse: not realizing people's impression of you *is* their reality of you. Your ability to socialize will either enhance or undermine your relationships in business or the community.

Second Gear – Connect

- Overuse: wanting everyone you meet to bare their soul to you, or sharing too many details about your life with others.
- Underuse: shallow or hollow relationships result from a shortage of undivided attention, expressing affection, and self-revelation.

First Gear – Recharge

- Overuse: having a preoccupation with your self-care that consumes too much time and infringes upon others.
- Underuse: self-care? What is that?

Reverse – Respond/Apologize

- Overuse: starting every sentence with, "Sorry..." Habitually taking responsibility for things beyond your fault or responsibility.
- Underuse: some people (some men?) have the mistaken idea that apologies show weakness and must be avoided at all costs.

What matters in life is not merely being exposed to new information but whether this information has gotten a hold of you and shaped your life!

The 5 Gears, like all GiANT's tools, are not presented merely for momentary amusement. The goal is to experience a profound improvement in your life by implementing these gears.

Please, don't think about these tools, hoping others are impressed by your knowledge. Demonstrate the use of these tools in your actions. It's what you *do* that counts!

Lord, there are so many things we as Christians read about and talk about but never do. *Keep us from this trap! Help us become* doers *of your Word and not hearers only. Help us become* doers *of these tools, too. Amen.*

Invincible

- Complete the Sherpa Training Session 19: 5 Gears Action Plan
- Video, 100 Exercise, and X Challenge

Involved

My child, pay attention to what I say.
Listen carefully to my words.
Don't lose sight of them.
Let them penetrate deep into your heart,
for they bring life to those who find them,
and healing to their whole body.
Guard your heart above all else,
for it determines the course of your life.
Avoid all perverse talk;
stay away from corrupt speech.
Look straight ahead,
and fix your eyes on what lies before you.
Mark out a straight path for your feet;
stay on the safe path.
Don't get sidetracked;
keep your feet from following evil.

—Proverbs 4:20–27 NLT (emphasis added)

Have you ever talked with someone, and it was clear their thoughts were somewhere else? Perhaps their eyes glazed over a bit as if they were tuned out. Or maybe their eyes were scanning the room looking for someone. They were standing right in front of you, but they were *not fully present*. I have had this experience many times. I am embarrassed to admit I have done it, too.

In such times, I neglected to extend the courtesy of fixing my gaze (attention) on them and what they were saying. I have also been offended when someone devalued what I was saying through this kind of behavior.

For some of us, an effective second or third gear would be our Learning Opportunity for our CORE Process. For others, it might be adjusting from the overuse or underuse of a gear.

What is my Learning Opportunity for the 5 Gears?

- *Call it*: In what situations ought I adjust, change, or respond differently?
- *Own it*: Why did it happen? What was my role in it?
- *Respond*: What will be my plan of *action*?
- *Execute*: What is my due date for getting this done? To whom will I be accountable?

Lord, help me pay attention to your voice. Turn my ear to the words you want me to hear. Help me take these tools and not let them out of my sight, but keep them in my mind. Let this wisdom bring health and success to my life. Guard my heart, for everything flows from it. Keep my mouth free of criticism, judgment, and negativity. Keep complaining and dishonest talk far from my lips. Let my eyes look straight ahead; fix my gaze directly before me. Help me give people the thoughtful attention they deserve. Empower me to be steadfast in all my ways, not turning to the right or the left; keep my feet from evil. Amen.

Invested

A. Please identify your vital insight from this session and write it in your *Breakthrough* Journal.

B. For reflection or discussion:

1. First Gear – Recharge: Do you overuse or underuse? What are the consequences?
2. Second Gear – Connect: Do you overuse or underuse? What are the consequences?
3. Third Gear – Social: Do you overuse or underuse? What are the consequences?
4. Fourth Gear – Tasks: Do you overuse or underuse? What are the consequences?
5. Fifth Gear – Focus: Do you overuse or underuse? What are the consequences?
6. Reverse – Respond/Apologize: Do you overuse or underuse? What are the consequences?
7. What is my Learning Opportunity when it comes to the 5 Gears?
8. Call it: In what situations ought I adjust, change, or respond differently?
9. Own it: Why did it happen? What was my role in it?
10. Respond: What will be my plan of action?
11. Execute: What is my due date for getting this done? To whom will I be accountable?

20

Liberating Others

INVITED

And in this way all Israel will be saved, as it is written:

The ***Liberator*** *will come from Zion;*
He will turn away godlessness from Jacob.
And this will be My covenant with them
when I take away their sins.

—Romans 11:26–27 HCSB (emphasis added)

Jesus is a *liberator* for humanity. Our focus this week and next is on what it might mean to be a *liberator* for those we lead. When asking what liberation is about, we discover several synonyms with overlapping meanings: *Liberator, Savior, Redeemer, Emancipator, Rescuer, Deliverer, Releaser.*

Note the implications of each:

- Liberator: free from domination
- Savior: save someone from danger

- Redeemer: compensate for 1) faults or bad aspects, or 2) unsatisfactory performance or behavior
- Emancipator: set free from legal, social, or political restrictions
- Rescuer: save someone from a dangerous or distressing situation
- Deliverer: save, rescue, or set someone or something free
- Releaser: allow or enable escape from confinement; set free

Take a moment and contemplate the following:

- How and when have you experienced these seven aspects of Jesus working in your life?
- Jesus's act of saving our souls by God's love and grace is the ultimate act of liberation. Think for a moment of people in your life who reflected God's grace to you, even in small ways.
- Who are the people that helped you along life's path in one of these seven aspects?
- How did they help you?

GiANT declares, "Liberators fight for the highest possible good in the lives of those they lead."

- What might it mean for you to become a liberator in the 5 Circles of Influence?
    - Liberating your self?
    - Liberating your family members?
    - Liberating your team?

- Liberating your organization?
- Liberating your community?

Great and wonderful Liberator, flow through me so that I might join you in your work of liberation. Point out to me the individuals in my circles of influence that I can help liberate. Teach me how to fight for their highest possible good. Amen.

Invincible

- Complete the Sherpa Training Session 20: Liberating Others
- Video, 100 Exercise, and X Challenge

Involved

> *As you go, proclaim this message: 'The kingdom of heaven has come near.' Heal the sick, raise the dead, cleanse those who have leprosy, drive out demons. Freely you have received; freely give.*
>
> —Matthew 10:7–8 NIV

Jesus is giving instructions to his disciples about the actions they ought to take. Likewise, GiANT's founder encouraged the GiANT team with these words:

> Always be open to taking a meeting from a referral or connector. Always be ready to serve others. You will be surprised what will come from those meetings. You may not make the sale, but because of the presence of Christ, the session will at least end in

healing, cleansing, casting out, or raising up some area of that individual's life.

Healing | Cleansing | Casting Out | Raising up

We may never be instruments of healing from cancer, but we can relieve pain, serve the vulnerable, and empower the weak.

We may never cleanse a leper, but we can offer grace, forgiveness, and the Savior who cleanses people from all manner of sin, guilt, shame, and degradation.

We may never perform an exorcism, but we can drive out fear, eliminate anger, banish hatred, evict prejudice, eject ignorance, get rid of loneliness, or cast down the idols of our day: money, power, greed, etc.

We may never raise the dead, but we can motivate the listless, inspire the downhearted, encourage the exhausted, urge the unresponsive, stir up faith, awaken hope, arouse love, create peace, and grow joy.

What do Liberators do as they fight for the highest possible good? They are healing, cleansing, casting out, and raising up—doing the works of the Kingdom of God by the power of God and for the glory of God (often without ever quoting a Bible verse or naming Jesus.) Liberators are letting the grace and goodness of God flow through them for the benefit of others. Liberators are conduits of God's blessing.

Lord, healing, cleansing, casting out, and raising up seem like your work and not mine. But you are within me, so I know this kind of liberation can happen. Let your liberating power flow through me to someone today. Amen.

Invested

A. Please identify your vital insight from this session and write it in your *Breakthrough* Journal.

B. For reflection or discussion:

Seven synonyms describe the ministry of Jesus: Liberator, Savior, Redeemer, Emancipator, Rescuer, Deliverer, Releaser.

Take a moment and contemplate the following:

1. How and when have you experienced these seven aspects of Jesus?
2. Who are the people that reflected one of these seven aspects of Jesus's ministry to you?
3. How did they help you?

GiANT declares *Liberators fight for the highest possible good in the lives of those they lead.* Consider what might it mean for you to be a liberator in the 5 Circles of Influence:

4. Liberating your self?
5. Liberating your family members?
6. Liberating your team?
7. Liberating your organization?
8. Liberating your community?
9. Share your thoughts about the concepts of healing, cleansing, casting out, and raising up.
10. What are some ways you do (or could) let the grace and goodness of God flow through you for the benefit of others?

21

Liberator's Intent

The Liberator's Intent Tool – Calling Up Instead of Calling Out

Invited

You will be doing the right thing if you obey the law of the Kingdom, which is found in the scripture, "Love your neighbor as you love yourself."

—James 2:8 GNT

"A new command I give you: Love one another. As I have loved you, so you must love one another. By this everyone will know that you are my disciples, if you love one another."

—John 13:34–35 NIV

> *In the light of eternity, we're here for a very short time, really. We're here for one thing, ultimately: to learn how to love, because God is love. Love is our origin, love is our ground, and love is our destiny.*
>
> —James Finley

In the earliest versions of GiANT, the tool read:

> *Love* means fighting for the highest possible good in the lives of those you lead.

Since most of our clients came from the male-dominated business world, it's not surprising GiANT received some feedback about promoting *love*. Nonetheless, isn't this a great definition?

Love is not merely warm feelings toward someone. Love takes action! Love is other-centered! And yes, love fights for the wellbeing of others!

Lord, make me a liberator who takes action on behalf of others and fights for their highest possible good. Amen.

Invincible

- Complete the Sherpa Training Session 21: The Liberator's Intent
- Video, 100 Exercise, and X Challenge

Involved

> *The Spirit of the Lord is on me, because he has anointed me to proclaim good news to the poor. He has sent me to proclaim freedom for the prisoners and recovery of sight for the blind, to set the oppressed free, to proclaim the year of the Lord's favor.*
>
> —Luke 4:18–19 NIV

When Jesus quotes the Old Testament prophet, he is declaring himself to be *the* liberator. In the same way that the moon reflects the light of the sun, how might we reflect the light of Jesus and become liberators?

Good news for the poor comes when we provide opportunities for them rather than judge them or blame victims.

So many people are locked away in prisons of the mind. We can proclaim freedom from the pain or trauma of how people or circumstances have damaged them. We can proclaim freedom from the guilt and shame of their own mistakes, blunders, sins, and wrongdoings.

In a world filled with con artists and falsehoods, we can overcome blindness by teaching people to discern truth and shine light into the darkness.

We can challenge the systems that perpetuate oppression, exploitation, and persecution—and work to set people free.

We will lift people out of habitual judgment and condemnation of self, others, and circumstances by proclaiming the love and grace of the Lord's favor!

Lord, I can't do it all, but I can do something. Reveal how you desire me to liberate my family, team, organization, and community. Amen.

Invested

A. Please identify your vital insight from this session and write it in your *Breakthrough* Journal.

B. For reflection or discussion:

1. What is your natural tendency: to call up or to call out?
2. In what situations have you experienced a superior as either "for me," "against me," or "for themself"?
3. How can you become someone who is consistently "for others"?
4. Jesus is *the* liberator. Just as the moon reflects the light of the sun, how might we reflect the light of Jesus and become liberators?
5. The poor often feel judged or blamed for their plight. What might we do to declare good news for the poor by providing opportunities for them?
6. So many people are locked away in prisons of the mind. How might we proclaim freedom from the pain or trauma from people or circumstances that have damaged them?
7. How might we proclaim freedom from the guilt and shame of their own mistakes, errors, blunders, sins, transgressions, and wrongdoings?
8. In a world filled with con artists and falsehoods, how might we overcome blindness by teaching people to discern the truth and by shining a light into their darkness?

9. How might we challenge the systems that perpetuate oppression, exploitation, and persecution—and work to set people free?
10. How might we lift people out of habitual judgment and condemnation of self, others, and circumstances by proclaiming the love and grace of the Lord's favor?

22

Communication Code: How to Communicate More Effectively

Invited

The wolf will live with the lamb,
the leopard will lie down with the goat,
the calf and the lion and the yearling together;
and a little child will lead them.
The cow will feed with the bear,
their young will lie down together,
and the lion will eat straw like the ox.
The infant will play near the cobra's den,
and the child will put its hand into the viper's nest.
They will neither harm nor destroy
on all my holy mountain,
for the earth will be filled with the knowledge of the Lord
as the waters cover the sea.

—Isaiah 11:6–9 NIV

This prophetic word gives hope for a future time when there will be no more fear, hostility, or danger. The human heart longs for a safe place to live and express ourselves.

Most people desire a safe place to think out loud and process thoughts or struggles now and then, merely wishing to be heard and understood.

The classic mistake occurs when a wife shares with her husband and simply wants someone to be with her, listen, and care. Then he responds with an action plan intended to "fix her problems." In Communication Code language, she needed Care, but he responded with Collaboration (at best) or, more likely, Critique.

The wife becomes frustrated because "he doesn't understand," while the husband is confused and thinking, "I offered the perfect solution to her problem!" Their different assessments of the kind of communication that would help leave the couple frustrated and at odds.

Lord, help me realize when the best thing I can do for someone is to sit with them, listen, and not offer any advice. Help me understand when care is required and when not speaking can speak volumes. Amen.

Invincible

- Complete the Sherpa Training Session 22: Communication Code Tendencies
- Video, 100 Exercise, and X Challenge

Involved

I will exalt you, my God the King;
I will praise your name for ever and ever.
Every day I will praise you
and extol your name for ever and ever.
Great is the LORD and most worthy of praise;
his greatness no one can fathom.

One generation commends your works to another;
they tell of your mighty acts.
They speak of the glorious splendor of your majesty—
and I will meditate on your wonderful works.
They tell of the power of your awesome works—
and I will proclaim your great deeds.
They ***celebrate*** *your abundant goodness*
and joyfully sing of your righteousness.

—Psalm 145:1–7 NIV, emphasis added

Throughout the Old Testament runs a theme of setting aside time to remember and celebrate God's action on Israel's behalf. In our daily lives, *celebration* strengthens relationships and builds people up.

In the Communication Code, asking someone to Celebrate is saying, "Will you take the time to celebrate [remember, observe, commemorate, honor, have fun, or rejoice] with me, and enjoy this accomplishment, achievement, or success?"

For many people empathizing with those who struggle comes easier than celebrating with those who are blessed. Why? Because the enemy is always there, tempting us into envy, or jealousy, or feeling bad about ourselves in comparison. That is why some people see Facebook as the "Bragbook," which may push a person toward sadness or depression. The posts make it appear like "everyone" else is happier, more popular, more prosperous, or having more fun than I am. What a trap!

I have started to say, "I am so happy for you!" when someone else is blessed or does well, and then I choose to rejoice with them. Their good fortune is no reflection on me. This is not a competition for the last cookie in the jar.

Let's build relationships by choosing to Celebrate the accomplishments and blessings of those around us.

Lord, thank you for blessing my colleagues and friends. Let me rejoice with total freedom at the good fortune they enjoy. Let me genuinely celebrate their hard-won accomplishments with them. Amen.

Invested

A. Please identify your vital insight from this session and write it in your *Breakthrough* Journal.

B. For reflection or discussion:

1. On a scale of 1–10 (ten being excellent), rate your skills with the following Communication Codes:
   a. Critique
   b. Collaborate
   c. Clarify
   d. Care
   e. Celebrate
2. Which one comes easily for you?
3. Which one is most elusive for you?
4. Which would you prefer to receive from others?
5. Which one would your family like more of from you?
6. Which one would your team like more of from you?
7. The prophetic word from Isaiah speaks of a safe place. How might we create more safe places for those in our lives?
8. How might we use the Care Code to "sit and listen" to the concerns of others?

9. In what ways might we intentionally generate the Celebration of little victories at work?
10. In what ways might we intentionally build in the Celebration of little victories with our family?

23

Communication Code: Your Challenges

Invited

> *Ask and it will be given to you; seek and you will find; knock and the door will be opened to you. For everyone who asks receives; the one who seeks finds; and to the one who knocks, the door will be opened.*
>
> —Matthew 7:7–8 NIV

When we seek the Clarify Communication Code, we are saying, "I've got something important brewing inside. Will you ask questions, pull out my thoughts, and help me clearly get my idea out on the table? Will you ask and listen well to gain a deep understanding of what is inside?"

Sometimes we have concerns inside and we want another person to *ask* gently and sincerely until we share with them. We wish for them to *seek* the hidden things in our thoughts that may be highly important but not readily available. We would like them to *knock* until they get our attention, and we open the door and invite them in.

Clients surveyed by GiANT most wished for someone to Clarify. They desired to experience the gift of dialogue with someone who has the skills and interest to ask, seek, and knock.

One of the most significant presents we can give another person is to *Clarify*—to truly hear and understand what they are trying to say!

This week, practice using Clarify as your first response. Intentionally seek greater understanding. Gently and lovingly ask and keep on asking.

Lord, help me learn to Clarify well. Give me the right questions to ask, the curiosity to be interested, the genuineness to appreciate what they have to say, and the persistence to gently open people. Let me help them express the wonders you have put into their lives. Grant me this good gift so I might use it to bless others. Amen.

Invincible

- Complete the Sherpa Training Session 23: Communication Code Challenges
- Video, 100 Exercise, and X Challenge

Involved

Blessed are those who find wisdom,
those who gain understanding,
for [wisdom] is more profitable than silver
and yields better returns than gold.

—Proverbs 3:13–14 NIV

Have you ever experienced teamwork with a partner in which the total was far greater than the sum of the parts? Sometimes the wisdom and understanding created by two people working in harmony produce results exponentially greater than two by themselves. The Collaborate communication code offers this possibility. The invitation to Collaborate says, "Here's my idea. I believe that with your added wisdom and understanding, we can create something incredible together. Join me. Let's work in partnership; let's cooperate and create something amazing."

Lord, give me wisdom and understanding to offer when someone asks me to Collaborate and grant me wisdom to ask for Collaboration when it would yield a better return than gold. Amen.

Invested

A. Please identify your vital insight from this session and write it in your *Breakthrough* Journal.

B. For reflection or discussion:

1. In what situations would it be helpful if someone would ask, seek, and knock until they fully understand what you mean?
2. Who in your world needs you to patiently draw out what they are thinking using the Clarify Code?
3. When, where, and how might this happen?
4. Tell about a time when you experienced "together is better" as you collaborated?
5. Who is your favorite collaboration partner? What factors made collaboration successful or enjoyable?
6. How might the Communication Code help you bring your best to your family?
7. How might the Communication Code help you bring your best to your work?

8. How might the Communication Code help you as a leader?
9. How might the Communication Code help you avoid potential communication breakdowns, blind spots, or landmines?

24

Communication Code: Active Listening Audit

Invited

> *Do not judge, or you too will be judged. For in the same way you judge others, you will be judged, and with the measure you use, it will be measured to you. Why do you look at the speck of sawdust in your brother's eye and pay no attention to the plank in your own eye? How can you say to your brother, 'Let me take the speck out of your eye,' when all the time there is a plank in your own eye? You hypocrite, first take the plank out of your own eye, and then you will see clearly to remove the speck from your brother's eye.*
>
> —Matthew 7:1–5 NIV

The *last* thing most people want is Critique—to be judged. Yet, something inside drives all human beings to judge. We judge ourselves; we judge others; we judge our circumstances. Habitual human judging makes many people anxious, frustrated, pessimistic, and miserable.

The Gospel encourages us to offer others grace instead of judgment—to love, bless, and build up others instead of tearing them down.

Critique (judging what we perceive as wrong) is often the first thing we do and the last thing they need. Nonetheless, there are times when we do want discernment from others. We want them to ask difficult questions and challenge assumptions to improve an idea or solution to a problem.

Seeking Critique is asking for discernment, not judgment. Some synonyms of critique include: review, assess, evaluate, examine, analyze, and scrutinize. The attitude offered is the key to effective Critique. Helpful Critique has the other's best interest at heart. Positive Critique does not tear them down, it builds them up.

Let's stop the habitual judging that is so often damaging or detrimental. Let's learn the art of discerning Critique that helps others learn, grow, and improves their plans or projects.

Lord, my thoughts so quickly and so often default to judgment. Help me learn the art of helpful Critique. Help me only to offer it when it is invited and would be beneficial. Amen.

Invincible

- Complete the Sherpa Training Session 24: Active Listening
- Video, 100 Exercise, and X Challenge

Involved

> *My dear brothers and sisters, take note of this: Everyone should be quick to listen, slow to speak and slow to become angry, because human anger does not produce the righteousness that God desires.*
>
> —James 1:19–20 NIV

It can be so frustrating when someone who "thinks they know" what you are going to say and reacts to what they think is coming without allowing you the opportunity to express what is on your mind. Sometimes they even jump to an angry response. Behavior like this harms communication and relationships. Yet this happens regularly to us, and we have done it to others too.

Perhaps we could excuse this behavior by acknowledging the brain processes information faster than a person can speak. The average speech rate for an American is about 125 words per minute; the human brain can process about 800 words per minute. The temptation to think ahead of the speaker is ever-present. We are processing our thoughts (and making judgments) about what we hear even before it entirely comes forth. But our brain capacity does not excuse bad or unhelpful behavior. It means we ought to be more disciplined and focus on listening and understanding before speaking.

- Are you a good listener?
- Do you seek to understand others?
- Do you ask helpful questions?
- Do you care about what others are trying to communicate?

Christ calls us to love one another. Love often means taking time to listen, care, and pay attention to what's happening.

Lord, help me be quick to listen, slow to speak, and slow to anger. Let me be an active and attentive listener who produces the righteousness you desire. Amen.

Invested

A. Please identify your vital insight from this session and write it in your *Breakthrough* Journal.

B. For reflection or discussion:

Harsh judgment comes naturally for humans as part of our fallen, sinful nature.

1. What is the difference between discernment and judgment?
2. In what situations do you judge yourself harshly?
3. In what situations do you judge others harshly?
4. In what situations do you judge your circumstances harshly?
5. How might we offer discerning critique without any harsh judgment?
6. How might it be helpful if we asked permission before offering a critique?
7. How well do you listen? Give examples of when you do well and when you don't.
8. How well do you seek to understand others?

9. How well do you ask helpful questions?
10. How much do you care about what others are trying to communicate?

25

CORE Process: Communication Code Action Plan

Invited

When they had finished eating, Jesus said to Simon Peter, "Simon son of John, do you love me more than these?"

"Yes, Lord," he said, "you know that I love you."

Jesus said, "Feed my lambs."

Again Jesus said, "Simon son of John, do you love me?"

He answered, "Yes, Lord, you know that I love you."

Jesus said, "Take care of my sheep."

The third time he said to him, "Simon son of John, do you love me?"

Peter was hurt because Jesus asked him the third time, "Do you love me?" He said, "Lord, you know all things; you know that I love you."

Jesus said, "Feed my sheep.

—John 21:15–17 NIV

After his resurrection, on the shores of the Sea of Galilee, Jesus clarifies love in action with Simon Peter. If we love God, we demonstrate love by our actions toward others.

Two of the ways GiANT describes love in action are:

1. Liberators fight for the highest possible good in the lives of those they lead.
2. Liberators calibrate both support and challenge [encouragement and accountability] to empower or provide opportunities for others.

A third way of describing love in action would be:

3. Liberators discern which Communication Code is most helpful for the person with whom they are in dialogue. Liberators clarify by asking or explaining which code will help both people converse on the same wavelength.

Love is not an ethereal feeling. Love in action meets the others' needs—tending to, caring for, and feeding people (God's sheep). Love is liberating and empowering others to become all God calls them to be.

Lord, empower me to fight for the highest possible good for others. Enable me to provide both support and challenge as required. Help me discern which Communication Code would be most helpful for this person at this time. Amen.

Invincible

- Complete the Sherpa Training Session 25: Communication Code Action Plan
- Video, 100 Exercise, and X Challenge

Involved

While he was still speaking, a bright cloud covered them, and a voice from the cloud said, "This is my Son, whom I love; with him I am well pleased. ***Listen to him****!"*

—Matthew 17:5 NIV, emphasis added

"The King will reply, 'Truly I tell you, whatever you did for one of the least of these brothers and sisters of mine, you did for me.'

—Matthew 25:40 NIV

God instructed the disciples to listen to Jesus, the beloved son. Jesus told the disciples whatever they do for the least deserving people, they are doing for the King of heaven.

How many times do others experience us as so busy we don't even want to listen? We assume we know what will be said or think what is coming is not worthy of our precious time.

Everyone would benefit if we would learn

- to listen.
- to listen to the Lord.
- to listen to people.
- to hear the Lord by listening to others.
- to serve the Lord by listening to others.

Lord, teach me to love and serve you by listening to others. Amen.

Invested

A. Please identify your vital insight from this session and write it in your *Breakthrough* Journal.

B. For reflection or discussion:

1. What is your learning opportunity for this week?
2. What steps would help you "marry self-awareness to action"?
3. What happened? Just the facts.
4. Why did it happen? What was your role in it?
5. What is your response/action plan/strategy to deal with it?
6. What is your deadline and accountability plan?
7. Peter was a fisherman, but Jesus asked him to "Feed my sheep"... why?
8. How might "fighting for the highest possible good" be love in action? Who needs you to fight for them?
9. How might calibrating support and challenge be love in action? Who needs support or challenge from you?
10. How might love in action involve discerning which communication code would be helpful? Who needs you to adjust your communication?
11. How might active listening be love in action? How might you serve the Lord by listening to others? Who needs you to listen?

26

Maximizing Influence: Building Trust

Invited

> *As soon as it was night, the believers sent Paul and Silas away to Berea. On arriving there, they went to the Jewish synagogue. Now the Berean Jews were of more noble character than those in Thessalonica, for they received the message with great eagerness and examined the Scriptures every day to see if what Paul said was true. As a result, many of them believed, as did also a number of prominent Greek women and many Greek men.*
>
> —Acts 17:10–12 NIV

The Bible describes the Jews of Berea as having a noble character. They searched for the truth and based their lives upon it. Doing so is the bedrock of honor, virtue, and morality. How can we build our lives on what is true and right and good?

The first step in building trust is demonstrating a noble character. There are tendencies among the 5 Voices that must be managed or overcome to build trust.

- The **Connector** voice often embodies immense passion and enthusiasm, but it can feel over the top. Sometimes it feels like the sales pitch of a used car salesman and sounds too good to be true. This voice may be perceived as promising more than can be delivered.
- The **Pioneer** voice is often so focused on accomplishing its mission that it comes across to the world with an attitude of "you only have value if you help me achieve my goals." The immature Pioneer is in danger of using people for their gain, and people wonder, "Is your being nice merely manipulative?"

People quickly become wary and cautious because somewhere in the past, they experienced someone who took advantage of them, and their defenses are up.

Whatever our voice, we would do well in personal relationships or business if we model after the Bereans who exhibited noble character.

Lord Jesus, help me build noble character traits based on your Word's truth and a loving relationship with you. Show me where to adjust my thinking, communication, and behavior to reflect your goodness, grace, and love toward others. Cleanse me of the selfishness that would tempt me to use others for my gain. Let me glorify you by serving others as I fight for the highest possible good in their lives. Amen.

Invincible

- Complete the Sherpa Training Session 26: Building Trust
- Video, 100 Exercise, and X Challenge

Involved

> *Love must be sincere. Hate what is evil; cling to what is good. Be devoted to one another in love. Honor one another above yourselves. Never be lacking in zeal, but keep your spiritual fervor, serving the Lord. Be joyful in hope, patient in affliction, faithful in prayer. Share with the Lord's people who are in need. Practice hospitality.*
>
> *Bless those who persecute you; bless and do not curse. Rejoice with those who rejoice; mourn with those who mourn. Live in harmony with one another. Do not be proud, but be willing to associate with people of low position. Do not be conceited.*
>
> *Do not repay anyone evil for evil. Be careful to do what is right in the eyes of everyone. If it is possible, as far as it depends on you, live at peace with everyone.*
>
> —Romans 12:9–18 NIV

Who wouldn't enjoy hanging out with people like that? What an excellent recipe for interpersonal chemistry! Relational chemistry is the second (of four) ingredients necessary to open the door to trust. Think of chemistry as harmony, likeability, and enjoying being together.

- Do people enjoy being with you?
- What factors in the passage above do you demonstrate that are attractive to others?
- And what factors might be a growth opportunity that would be helpful for you to embody?

Of our 5 Voices, these may have tendencies that diminish chemistry:

- The **Creative-Pioneer** may exhibit some social awkwardness, possibly snarky, reserved, or passive-aggressive behavior. Learn to share your thoughts and ideas in a pleasant and likable way.
- **Guardians** tend to trade in the currency of transaction and information. They would benefit by intentionally building mutually beneficial relationships. Showing a little emotion (some humanity and vulnerability) might help a lot.
- If **Pioneers** fall into the trap (tendency) of valuing only people who can help them conquer the next big goal, others may perceive this as arrogance and a lack of concern for others.

Paul's list for creating chemistry is extensive: sincere love, clinging to good, honor, devotion to one another, joy, hope, patience, faithfulness, empathy, harmony, humility, doing right, and living at peace. Who wouldn't enjoy having people like this as friends, clients, or co-workers?

Lord Jesus, is there anything in my life that repels people from wanting to connect with me? I know your life flows through relationships. Make me the kind of person who has positive chemistry with others. Let me be trustworthy and winsome for the sake of your Kingdom. Amen.

Invested

A. Please identify your vital insight from this session and write it in your *Breakthrough* Journal.

B. For reflection or discussion:

Character + Chemistry + Competency + Credibility = Trust

1. What are your thoughts about this equation?
2. With which of the four filters do you tend to lead? What do you value most?
3. What might be your area of growth?
4. How might you become more intentional about how you build trust with your people?
5. Luke describes the Bereans as having a noble character. Why might people say that about you? Why not?
6. In a fallen world supporting the idea that "it's OK to say anything to win," how important are truth, honor, virtue, and morality to you personally?
7. Why might people enjoy being with you? In what situations might they not?
8. What factors in the Romans 12 passage do you demonstrate that are attractive to others?
9. What factors might be a growth opportunity that would be helpful for you to embody?
10. What are your action items for this session?

27

Maximizing Influence: 5 Voices Connection

Invited

Are we beginning to commend ourselves again? Or do we need, like some people, letters of recommendation to you or from you? You yourselves are our letter, written on our hearts, known and read by everyone. You show that you are a letter from Christ, the result of our ministry, written not with ink but with the Spirit of the living God, not on tablets of stone but on tablets of human hearts.

Such confidence we have through Christ before God. Not that we are competent in ourselves to claim anything for ourselves, but our competence comes from God. He has made us competent as ministers of a new covenant—not of the letter but of the Spirit; for the letter kills, but the Spirit gives life.

—2 Corinthians 3:1–6 NIV

Here Paul is claiming competence of his ministry, his message, and his methods. He claims no need to tell others how well he has done or rely on others' recommendation letters. He depends on the results of the ministry—the evidence of transformed lives speaks louder than words.

When people evaluate our competency, they measure:

- skills and proficiency,
- understanding and expertise, and
- knowledge-based action that gets results.

When looking at 5 Voices' tendencies, which Voices might not readily project competency?

- The **Nurturer** may have a "competency perception" deficiency if others see you as too people-centered and enough not skills-oriented. Or you may not be good at revealing your competency. Don't hide what you do well!
- The **Creative-Connector** may be thinking so far ahead of others they "don't get you," or you may have trouble expressing your helpful ideas and demonstrating your value to the team.
- The **Connector** may experience a competence gap if people are concerned you may over-promise and underdeliver.

For all of us, life is a tight rope walk of demonstrating our strengths and competencies to others without "beginning to commend ourselves," boasting, or appearing arrogant. May we allow the good results of our competencies to speak for themselves.

Lord Jesus, help us be both competent and humble, letting the results of our strengths and hard work speak for themselves. Show us how to demonstrate genuine competency that will help us build trust with others. Amen.

Invincible

- Complete the Sherpa Training Session 27: Maximizing Influence / 5 Voices Connection
- Video, 100 Exercise, and X Challenge

Involved

Whoever can be trusted with very little can also be trusted with much, and whoever is dishonest with very little will also be dishonest with much. So if you have not been trustworthy in handling worldly wealth, who will trust you with true riches? And if you have not been trustworthy with someone else's property, who will give you property of your own?

—Luke 16:10–12 NIV

Job interviewers always ask about how you performed in certain situations in the past. The assumption is past performance predicts future results. This passage declares trustworthiness, honesty, and competency in little things will predict how one will handle much bigger things. Credibility involves not only those three elements but includes one more. The other person is asking about you, "Can you take what you know and create a tailor-made solution for my unique problem?"

Credibility is utilizing character and competency to understand another person's situation and solve their issue or concern. If you can do that in the little things, there are no limits on what you can handle!

Lord Jesus, grant me wisdom and insights into what people need from me. Help me understand their situation and use all the resources You have provided to meet their need. Amen.

Invested

A. Please identify your vital insight from this session and write it in your *Breakthrough* Journal.

B. For reflection or discussion:

1. How might a Nurturer overcome a "competency perception deficiency" if others see them as too people-centered and not skills-oriented enough?
2. How might a Nurturer overcome their "soft voice" tendency that hides their incredible competency and credibility?
3. How might the Creative-Connector overcome their natural tendencies of thinking so far ahead of others that people don't follow? Or overcome their difficulty asserting their valuable ideas to the team?
4. How might the Creative-Pioneer overcome a tendency for some social awkwardness, possibly snarky, reserved, or passive-aggressive behavior?
5. How might Guardians overcome their tendency to trade in the currency of transaction and information rather than building mutually beneficial relationships?
6. How might the enthusiastic Connector overcome sounding like the sales pitch of a "used car salesman" that sounds too good to be true?

7. How might Pioneers avoid falling into the trap (tendency) of valuing only people who can help them conquer the next big goal?

8. How might Pioneers overcome the danger of using people for their gain and causing people to wonder, "Are you being nice to me in an attempt to manipulate me?"

9. Who in your family or team might benefit from understanding how they would gain from growing in one of these four components necessary for building trust? How might you help them succeed in this area?

10. Credibility arises when someone uses character and competency to understand another person's situation and solve their issues. That's what makes you relevant to people. How good are you at understanding the concerns of others and helping them solve their problems?

28

Maximizing Influence: Overcoming Self Preservation

Invited

> *But when Peter came to Antioch, I had to stand up against him because he was guilty. Peter had been eating with the people who are not Jews. But after some men came who had been with James, he kept away from them. He was afraid of those who believe in the religious act of becoming a Jew. Then the rest of the Jews followed him because they were afraid to do what they knew they should do.*
>
> —Galatians 2:11–13a NLV

Peter witnessed a vision of God, inviting him to eat all manner of food, including what he was not allowed to eat because of religious rules. The voice spoke to him: "Do not call anything impure that God has made clean"(Acts 10:15). Peter thus realized the message and ministry of Christ was not only for the Jews. Thus Peter began eating with people who are not Jews. But he quickly backtracked when he was afraid of some men who had been with James. Paul stood up against Peter's behavior in the passage above.

What was Peter afraid of losing?

- Perhaps his reputation?
- Perhaps his popularity?
- People's opinion of him?

Had James's emissaries brought word there was a fresh outburst of persecution from the Jewish authorities? The early church splintered into factions with significant political and theological differences and faced dangers American Christians can't understand. But Peter became afraid. His fear spread among his followers and kept them from doing what was right.

So what are you afraid of losing? We learn today how self-preservation is often overprotection of something you fear losing. It causes us to behave in ways that have a negative impact not only on us but on those around us. We discover the fear of losing can cause loss—often the loss of the very thing we are concerned about losing.

Lord Jesus, there are things I am afraid of losing. Help me entrust these things and all of my life into your hands. I surrender all of my life to you, and I trust you to take care of anything I might fear losing. Shift my heart and mind from fear to faith—from fear to the perfect love that casts out fear. Whenever I am afraid, I will trust in God. Amen.

Invincible

- Complete the Sherpa Training Session 28: Overcoming Self Preservation
- Video, 100 Exercise, and X Challenge

Involved

[The kingdom of heaven] will be like a man going on a journey, who called his servants and entrusted his wealth to them. To one he gave five bags of gold, to another two bags, and to another one bag, each according to his ability. Then he went on his journey. The man who had received five bags of gold went at once and put his money to work and gained five bags more. So also, the one with two bags of gold gained two more. But the man who had received one bag went off, dug a hole in the ground and hid his master's money.

After a long time the master of those servants returned and settled accounts with them. The man who had received five bags of gold brought the other five. 'Master,' he said, 'you entrusted me with five bags of gold. See, I have gained five more.' His master replied, 'Well done, good and faithful servant! You have been faithful with a few things; I will put you in charge of many things. Come and share your master's happiness!' The man with two bags of gold also came. 'Master,' he said, 'you entrusted me with two bags of gold; see, I have gained two more.' His master replied, 'Well done, good and faithful servant! You have been faithful with a few things; I will put you in charge of many things. Come and share your master's happiness!'

Then the man who had received one bag of gold came. 'Master,' he said, 'I knew that you are a hard man, harvesting where you have not sown and gathering where you have not scattered seed. So I was afraid and went out and hid your gold in the ground. See, here is what belongs to you.'

His master replied, 'You wicked, lazy servant! So you knew that I harvest where I have not sown and gather where I have not scattered seed? Well then, you should

> *have put my money on deposit with the bankers, so that when I returned I would have received it back with interest. So take the bag of gold from him and give it to the one who has ten bags. For whoever has will be given more, and they will have an abundance. Whoever does not have, even what they have will be taken from them.*
>
> —Matthew 25: 14–29 NIV

What was wrong with this guy? How could he be so stupid? It makes sense to put the money in the bank and at least gain interest.

It is easy to stand back and criticize. Perhaps a few benevolent souls might be empathetic enough to wonder what kind of damage this person received in his life that made him so dysfunctional. The bottom line is he was afraid. Fear paralyzed him. And it got him into trouble.

When I started consulting, I was trying to hide my lack of experience. I had recently been trained and had only delivered the content in volunteer settings. I was trying to hide my lack of professional experience. Some say that dogs can smell fear, but this prospect didn't like the fear he smelled on me and asked for another consultant to handle his account. The next time, I partnered with a qualified consultant, landed the client, and gained confidence and competence.

What are you trying to hide? Of what are you afraid? Get honest with yourself about this. Get real with God. Let God help you become a leader who is secure, confident, and humble. Humility is the willingness to be known for who you are with no fear and nothing to hide.

Lord Jesus, it's time to stop hiding the valuable things you have given me. Rid me of the fear that paralyzes me so I will quit hiding. Turn me into a servant who will double your investments and make you happy. Amen.

Invested

A. Please identify your vital insight from this session and write it in your *Breakthrough* Journal.

B. For reflection or discussion:

1. How did Peter's fear keep him from the freedom God had shown him?
2. How did Peter's fear hinder the work of the Gospel?
3. What are you afraid of losing?
4. What are you trying to hide?
5. What are you trying to prove (and to whom)?
6. Is there anything limiting you where you can't get out of your way?
7. How can fear cause us to behave in ways that have a negative impact not only on us but on those around us?
8. Explain how the fear of losing can often cause loss—usually of the very thing we are concerned about losing?
9. In what situation might you have felt "paralyzed" by fear? What happened? What helped?
10. What is God's plan for getting rid of your fear?

29

Maximizing Influence: Relationship Before Opportunity

Invited

Therefore if you have any encouragement from being united with Christ, if any comfort from his love, if any common sharing in the Spirit, if any tenderness and compassion, then make my joy complete by being like-minded, having the same love, being one in spirit and of one mind. Do nothing out of selfish ambition or vain conceit. Rather, in humility value others above yourselves, not looking to your own interests but each of you to the interests of the others.

In your relationships with one another, have the same mindset as Christ Jesus:

Who, being in very nature God, did not consider equality with God something to be used to his own advantage; rather, he made himself nothing by taking the very nature of a servant, being made in human likeness. And being found in appearance as a man, he humbled himself by becoming obedient to death—even death on a cross!

—Philippians 2:1–8 NIV

In your relationships with one another… This phrase ties together everything that comes before and after in this passage. What comes before? Encouragement, comfort, love, tenderness, compassion, joy, unity, humility, and looking to others' interests. *Wow!* Sounds amazing enough. Can't we leave it there? But Paul goes on, have the same mindset as Christ Jesus, who made himself nothing, became a servant, humbled himself, was obedient, and died on a cross.

We would be delighted to ask the Spirit for all those good things at the top. Most of the time, we want to believe Jesus suffered and died, so we would never have pain, sorrow, or difficulties in our lives. But a theology of glory is balanced in Scriptures with a theology of the cross that calls us to take up our cross and bear others' burdens.

People do not exist to be used for our gain. Instead, they provide us with an opportunity to "fight for the highest possible good in the lives of others." The Christian calling is to love, serve, care for, and improve the lives of others. Real opportunity flows out of the relationship.

Lord Jesus, when I look at other people, help me see potential relationships where I can be a blessing to others. Open the right kind of possibilities out of these mutually-beneficial relationships that might bear fruit for your kingdom. Amen.

Invincible

- Complete the Sherpa Training Session 29: Relationship before Opportunity
- Video, 100 Exercise, and X Challenge

Involved

> *On the seventh day, they got up at daybreak and marched around the city seven times in the same manner, except that on that day they circled the city seven times. The seventh time around, when the priests sounded the trumpet blast, Joshua commanded the army, "Shout! For the LORD has given you the city... When the trumpets sounded, the army shouted, and at the sound of the trumpet, when the men gave a loud shout, the wall collapsed; so everyone charged straight in, and they took the city.*
>
> —Joshua 6:15–16, 20 NIV

People build walls for protection, and the walls of Jericho were tall and strong. But God gave the Israelites what seemed like a ridiculous plan. Yet when they obeyed, the walls came tumbling down.

We build emotional walls for self-protection. Then God seemingly gives us a ridiculous plan. Check the traffic light at the top of the wall and when the time, place, and person are right, take down your walls. Taking down walls leaves us vulnerable, but it is the pathway to move beyond a transaction to a relationship. Hopefully, once we drop our wall, the other person will drop theirs, and we can establish a meaningful relationship.

If you want to live on the relational side of influence and impact, you have to practice lowering your wall and inviting the other person to lower their self-preservation wall.

Lord Jesus, grant me wisdom to see the signals atop my wall. Grant me the courage to lower my wall when the time is right. Grant me the grace to accept my sister or brother that lowers their wall before me.

Grant us the gift of a relationship with impact and influence guided by your presence. Amen.

Invested

A. Please identify your vital insight from this session and write it in your *Breakthrough* Journal.

B. For reflection or discussion:

1. What is unbalanced about the "theology of glory" that says Christ has suffered so we might have ongoing health and prosperity?
2. What may be unbalanced about the "theology of the cross" that invites us to join in the sufferings of Christ on behalf of the world?
3. How can we hold these two together and live in the tension between them?
4. How can we live our lives *for* God and *for* others instead of thinking that God and others exist purely for our benefit?
5. What factors lead to fear of taking down our walls of self-protection?
6. How are vulnerability and honesty the foundation for a genuine relationship?
7. What are we missing in life when we live behind the walls of self-preservation?
8. How shall we discern when and with whom to take down our walls?

9. Why is a relationship more valuable than a transaction?
10. What could you do that would leave a legacy of positive influence and impact?

30

CORE Process: Maximizing Influence

Invited

I hope in the Lord Jesus to send Timothy to you soon, that I also may be cheered when I receive news about you. I have no one else like him, who will show genuine concern for your welfare. For everyone looks out for their own interests, not those of Jesus Christ. But you know that Timothy has proved himself, because as a son with his father he has served with me in the work of the gospel. I hope, therefore, to send him as soon as I see how things go with me. And I am confident in the Lord that I myself will come soon.

—Philippians 2:19–24 NIV

Timothy proved himself showing genuine concern for Philippi's believers and how he served with Paul in the gospel's work. Therefore Paul trusted him and was happy to send Timothy as his representative.

Like Timothy, people can prove themselves out of a motivation of loving God and others. Or people can try to prove themselves out of fear. The question is: what are you trying to prove? To whom? Are your motivations coming from love or fear? It makes all the difference in the world.

Lord Jesus, free me from trying to prove myself out of fear. This kind of proof is never enough, and the tentacles of fear never let go. Let me be comfortable in my skin with nothing to prove at all. Or else let me prove myself out of love for you and others. Amen.

Invincible

- Complete the Sherpa Training Session 30: Maximizing Influence Action Plan
- Video, 100 Exercise, and X Challenge

Involved

> *Above all, love each other deeply, because love covers over a multitude of sins. Offer hospitality to one another without grumbling. Each of you should use whatever gift you have received to serve others, as faithful stewards of God's grace in its various forms. If anyone speaks, they should do so as one who speaks the very words of God. If anyone serves, they should do so with the strength God provides, so that in all things God may be praised through Jesus Christ. To him be the glory and the power for ever and ever. Amen.*
>
> —1 Peter 4:8–11 NIV

Each of you should use whatever gift you have received to serve others… If you have the gift of leadership, then become a servant leader.

Servant leadership is a leadership philosophy in which the leader's primary goal is to serve—or perhaps to "fight for the highest possible good for those they lead." Traditional leadership generally involves the accumulation and exercise of power by one at the "top of the pyramid." Servant leadership turns the pyramid upside down and focuses primarily on the growth and well-being of those led.

As a servant leader, you focus on your team and how your efforts can help them succeed and do their best work. You have to stop thinking about yourself and start learning about your team. It's also about changing your mindset for success. The servant leader takes responsibility to ensure everyone in the group moves upward. The result is a happier, more effective, and productive team, and performance improves accordingly.

Maximizing influence is not only valuable with your prospects and vendors; it is essential with those you lead. Everyone in your organization is looking to see whether you embody the four elements necessary to create trust:

1. Character
2. Chemistry
3. Competency
4. Credibility

And everyone in the organization is looking to see whether you use people for your success or whether you define success as the sum of everyone's success on your team. Servant leadership that calibrates support and challenge creates a culture of empowerment and opportunities. When a leader can appropriately express vulnerability and lower their walls, the team has the potential to become a "family" of relationships that can be both highly rewarding and incredibly productive.

BREAKTHROUGH

Dear Lord,
Leadership is hard to define.
Lord, let us be the ones to define it with justice.
Leadership is like a handful of water.
Lord, let us be the people to share it with those who thirst.
Leadership is not about watching and correcting.
Lord, let us remember it is about listening and connecting.
Leadership is not about telling people what to do.
Lord, let us find out what people want.
Leadership is less about the love of power,
and more about the power of love.

Lord, as we continue to undertake the leader role, let us affirm the servant leadership we witness in your son Jesus.
Let us walk in the path he has set and follow in his footsteps.

Let our greatest passion be compassion.
Our greatest strength, love.
Our greatest victory, the reward of peace.

In leading let us never fail to follow.
In loving let us never fail.
Amen.

—Anonymous

Invested

A. Please identify your vital insight from this session and write it in your *Breakthrough* Journal.

B. For reflection or discussion:

1. People can either prove themselves out of a motivation of loving or out of fear. What are you trying to prove? To whom?
2. Are your motivations coming from love or fear? Talk about this.
3. How might you use your gifts as a servant-leader?
4. What would be different in your workplace if the primary goal of leadership were to build the whole by fighting for the highest possible good of those involved?
5. Individuals and companies' fortunes throughout history have amassed all too often by using and even abusing others. How might it be possible to be successful and also Christlike?
6. How might the four elements necessary to create trust benefit your prospects, your vendors, and those you lead?
7. Everyone is looking to see whether you use people for your success or define success as the sum of everyone's success on your team. How might servant leadership bring even greater success in an organization that you know?
8. What might change if a leader appropriately expresses vulnerability and lowers their walls, and the team

becomes a "family" of rewarding and productive relationships?

9. How might servant leadership calibrate support and challenge to create a culture of empowerment and opportunities?
10. What other GiANT tools and teachings of the past six months might help foster Christ-like leadership?

31

How to Develop Others Effectively

Invited

Have two goals: wisdom—that is, knowing and doing right—and common sense. Don't let them slip away, for they fill you with living energy and bring you honor and respect.

—Proverbs 3:21–22 TLB

This Proverb defines competence worth considering as we motivate our charges around the Apprenticeship Square. Incompetence comes either from a lack of common sense or a lack of knowing and doing right. Both need to be challenged for people to gain success-producing skills.

What would it mean in your setting and with your team to foster both wisdom and common sense? Are these terms they would use to describe you? Remember, we can only impart to others the skills and character traits we embody.

Lord Jesus, open my eyes to see the truth. Open my ears to hear your word. I open my heart to gain understanding and your eternal divine wisdom along with common sense. Help me be a blessing to others and develop them to become all you have in mind for them to be. Amen.

Invincible

- Complete the Sherpa Training Session 31: How to Develop Others Effectively
- Video, 100 Exercise, and X Challenge

Involved

> *May our Lord Jesus Christ himself and God our Father, who loved us and by his grace gave us eternal encouragement and good hope, encourage your hearts and strengthen you in every good deed and word.*
>
> —2 Thessalonians 2: 16–17 NIV

The pit of despair is an all-too-common experience. When people struggle to learn a new skill, they feel incompetent and tempted to give up. If someone you lead is in the pit and you withdraw, they are trapped.

Here is where they require encouragement and hope. Remind them of the vision that started them on this journey. Spend time with them, giving support and letting them know you believe in them. Recall those who encouraged you along life's pathway, and pass on the blessing. Remember how Jesus Christ loves you and gives you "eternal encouragement and good hope." Use this to help strengthen the heart of your protégé.

Lord Jesus, let my words always benefit and encourage those who hear them. Help me see if someone is in the pit of despair. Let me be the ladder of reassurance and inspiration they can climb to be fully released. Amen.

Invested

A. Please identify your vital insight from this session and write it in your Breakthrough *Journal.*

B. For reflection or discussion:

1. What would it mean in your setting and with your team to foster wisdom and common sense?
2. Would your team describe you as displaying wisdom and common sense?
3. Do you have an intentional process for developing others?
4. Do you have a way to determine where they are on the Apprenticeship Square?
5. How have you responded when one of your people fell into the pit of despair?
6. How might you do a better job of sharing relational time, vision, and encouragement with a struggling person?
7. Think about your team (or family or other settings). What skillsets are you developing in those under your care?
8. Choose one person and assess where they are on the square.
9. What does that person require from you right now?
10. When has God or a person infused you with their encouragement and hope for your future? How might you share this with others?

32

The Responsive Leader

Invited

> *Do nothing out of selfish ambition or vain conceit. Rather, in humility value others above yourselves, not looking to your own interests but each of you to the interests of the others.*
>
> —Philippians 2:3–4 NIV

We look at several dichotomies this week, including:

- Insecure vs. Secure
- Arrogant vs. Confident
- Prideful vs. Humble
- Resistant vs. Responsive

When the Holy Spirit shines the light of truth deep into the crevasses of our lives, what we see may not be pleasant. None of us wants to admit selfishness, vanity, ambition, or conceit turns our interests inward when we ought to turn Godward and otherward.

Humility is not weak. It takes strength to be willing to be known for who you are. It takes tremendous strength:

- to sweep away selfish pride and fight for the highest possible good in the lives of those we lead,
- to be receptive to opportunities for growth and change, and
- to be responsive, secure, confident, and humble.

No one is perfect in these matters. We are all on a journey of self-improvement by God's grace and power.

Lord Jesus, I am far too often influenced by what others think of me. I am always pretending to be richer, smarter, or nicer than I am. Please prevent me from trying to attract attention. Don't let me gloat about praise or be discouraged by criticism. Nor let me waste time weaving imaginary situations in which the most heroic, charming, and witty person present is myself. Show me how to be humble of heart, like you. Amen. (author unknown)

Invincible

- Complete the Sherpa Training Session 32: The Responsive Leader
- Video, 100 Exercise, and X Challenge

Involved

As for God, his way is perfect:
The LORD's word is flawless;
he shields all who take refuge in him.
For who is God besides the LORD?
And who is the Rock except our God?
It is God who arms me with strength
and keeps my way secure.

—Psalm 18:30–32 NIV

Insecure leaders are often on the defensive and resistant to learning about their blind spots. Insecurity blocks their growth as well as their relationships with others. How excellent that we don't have to conjure up our sense of wellbeing. It is God who is our source of security. God will shield us when we take refuge in Him. God will arm us with strength and keep our way secure. That sets us free from self-consciousness or fear and allows us to be responsive to others.

Dear Lord, be my security and fill my heart with peace. Make me stand firm in your faithfulness and fulfill your purpose for my life. Let me never feel threatened or defensive when someone tells the truth about one of my growth opportunities. Let me be responsive to the voice of your Spirit to adjust my thinking, words, and behavior so I might better give you glory and bless others. Amen.

Invested

A. Please identify your vital insight from this session and write it in your *Breakthrough* Journal.

B. For reflection or discussion:

1. Where do you fall on the spectrum between humility and "vain conceit"? How has this changed over the years?
2. When are you most confident or least confident?
3. How secure are you in your abilities a) to do your work? b) to develop meaningful relationships?
4. In what situations are you comfortable owning your weaknesses?
5. What kinds of challenges trigger your defensiveness?

6. Which word-pair describes your growth opportunity?

   a. Insecure vs. Secure
   b. Arrogant vs. Confident
   c. Prideful vs. Humble
   d. Resistant vs. Responsive

7. What might help you draw even greater security from the Lord?

8. What is your request of God at this time?

9. In what ways are you pretending?

10. How might you put this tool to work in a current situation?

33

Investing Time Intentionally

Invited

As they were walking along the road, a man said to him, "I will follow you wherever you go."

Jesus replied, "Foxes have dens and birds have nests, but the Son of Man has no place to lay his head."

He said to another man, "Follow me." But he replied, "Lord, first let me go and bury my father."

Jesus said to him, "Let the dead bury their own dead, but you go and proclaim the kingdom of God."

Still another said, "I will follow you, Lord; but first let me go back and say goodbye to my family."

Jesus replied, "No one who puts a hand to the plow and looks back is fit for service in the kingdom of God."

—Luke 9: 57–62 NIV

Jesus didn't seem like a formal kind of guy. But there were times when great crowds gathered, and Jesus spoke to them in a "formal" setting. The Sermon on the Mount would be an example.

Yet much of Jesus's training of his disciples happened informally "as they were walking along the road." They would see a need, and Jesus would meet it. Someone with a hurt would call out, and Jesus would heal it. Someone would ask a question, and Jesus would answer it. Jesus used the situation in front of him as a teaching moment.

We can also use formal settings and current informal concerns as teaching opportunities for those we lead either at work or home.

Lord, thank you for the opportunity to influence those in our charge. You always have a divine plan. We love you for that, Father. We celebrate how even when we have done what you have asked; the results are much more excellent than we could have imagined.

Our prayer today is that your will be done in our relationships at home and work. Take what we have prepared and multiply our efforts as only you can. Steer our intentions to align with your righteous will. Remind us of your faithful provision when our efforts fail us or fall short. May all glory go to you when we reach the finish line and climb over benchmarks. Blanket us with your peace today, Father. Keep us physically safe and guard our hearts and minds against pride and selfishness. May love be the guiding light for all we set out to accomplish and celebrate. Amen.

Invincible

- Complete the Sherpa Training Session 33: Investing Time Intentionally
- Video, 100 Exercise, and X Challenge

Involved

> *As Jesus and his disciples were leaving Jericho, a large crowd followed him. Two blind men were sitting by the roadside, and when they heard that Jesus was going by, they shouted, "Lord, Son of David, have mercy on us!"*

> *The crowd rebuked them and told them to be quiet, but they shouted all the louder, "Lord, Son of David, have mercy on us!"*
>
> *Jesus stopped and called them. "What do you want me to do for you?" he asked.*
>
> *"Lord," they answered, "we want our sight."*
>
> *Jesus had compassion on them and touched their eyes. Immediately they received their sight and followed him.*
>
> —Matthew 20:29–34 NIV

Jesus never gave a formal seminar on "how to heal the sick;" he healed as the opportunity arose. Jesus never codified the "10 steps to caring for people;" he demonstrated compassion for them. Most of the encounters captured in the Gospels are unique, as if there exists no *right way* to do God's will and serve people.

What's more, Jesus did not teach his disciples the fine points of doing religious acts. Jesus modeled how to love, live, and let heaven break into our daily lives.

May we also invest our lives discipling those God has entrusted into our care at work, at home, and in the community. Don't worry about the *right way to do it.* Genuinely listen to the needs calling out around you and reach out to help.

Lord Jesus, discipling is such a religious word that we often don't identify those you have given us to disciple—to care for, teach, or train. Sometimes formal and structured lessons or feedback is most helpful. Sometimes informal and spontaneous interaction works best. Help us to calibrate the two and strategically invest time in those you have given us. Amen.

Invested

A. Please identify your vital insight from this session and write it in your *Breakthrough* Journal.

B. For reflection or discussion:

1. Which is more natural for you, structured or spontaneous interactions?
2. What would increase balance in this dynamic?
3. What person on your team will benefit when you invest strategically in them?
4. What is their current learning opportunity?
5. What person in your family will benefit when you invest strategically in them?
6. What is their current learning opportunity?
7. Would additional formal or informal time with them be most beneficial?
8. What would it mean to invest your time more strategically for the sake of others?
9. How would strategically investing your time for others glorify God?
10. How would investing in others impact your faith development and relationship with Christ?

34

Setting Clear Expectations

Invited

> *I want to suggest that you finish what you started to do a year ago, for you were not only the first to propose this idea, but the first to begin doing something about it. Having started the ball rolling so enthusiastically, you should carry this project through to completion just as gladly, giving whatever you can out of whatever you have. Let your enthusiastic idea at the start be equaled by your* ***realistic*** *action now.*
>
> —2 Corinthians 8:10–11 TLB (emphasis added)

Realistic is the key! Unreasonable expectations in the business world are a leading cause of damaging stress for workers. Many children are traumatized by an authority figure burdening them with unrealistic and impossible expectations. Many pastors and other leaders have been raked over the coals because they could not meet the group's unrealistic or unattainable expectations.

On the other end of the spectrum, lives can be stunted in various ways if those around them hold them back or push them down with limited or resigned expectations. Either way is unhealthy. Realistic expectations are a necessary ingredient for creating a healthy culture.

What about you? What situations or people placed inappropriate and unhelpful expectations on you? How did you deal with it? Have you overcompensated? Can you discern the boundaries of healthy, realistic expectations?

Lord Jesus, thank you that any inappropriate expectations others may have of me don't automatically hurt or limit my life. Help me draw healthy and clear boundaries for what I can and cannot do. Help me calibrate support and challenge by providing realistic expectations for those around me. Amen.

Invincible

- Complete the Sherpa Training Session 34: Setting Clear Expectations
- Video, 100 Exercise, and X Challenge

Involved

> *Oh, that you would burst forth from the skies and come down! How the mountains would quake in your presence! The consuming fire of your glory would burn down the forests and boil the oceans dry. The nations would tremble before you; then your enemies would learn the reason for your fame! So it was before when you came down, for you did awesome things beyond our highest expectations, and how the mountains quaked! For since the world began no one has seen or heard of such a God as ours, who works for those who wait for him!*
>
> —Isaiah 64:1–4 TLB

Let's get real. God is the only being in the universe who can do "awesome things beyond our highest expectations." It has been said, "To be human is to be beautifully flawed." We all have strengths and weaknesses, the potential to create tremendous good or tremendous harm. If we place expectations on others that are too high, we harm them by publicly exposing their shortcomings. If our expectations for them are too low, we impede their strengths. Neither extreme is helpful to others, nor is it godly.

Lord Jesus, help me set realistic expectations for myself, my family, and my team. Let me be a liberator who empowers others and provides appropriate opportunities for them. Remind me how setting realistic expectations is part of fighting for the highest possible good for others. Amen.

Invested

A. Please identify your vital insight from this session and write it in your *Breakthrough* Journal.

B. For reflection or discussion:

1. What situations or people have placed inappropriate and unhelpful expectations on you?
2. How have you dealt with it?
3. Have you overcompensated?
4. Can you discern the boundaries of healthy, realistic expectations?
5. Are you good at setting realistic expectations for yourself, your family, and your team?

6. Is your tendency to set expectations too high or too low?
7. In what setting do you see roles that need clarification?
8. In what setting are there tasks that need clarification?
9. In what setting do you see responsibilities that need clarification?
10. How can you create a collaborative effort to define these aspects of relationships more clearly?

35

CORE Process: The Intentional Transfer Plan

Invited

> *Do you not know that in a race all the runners run, but only one gets the prize? Run in such a way as to get the prize. Everyone who competes in the games goes into strict training. They do it to get a crown that will not last, but we do it to get a crown that will last forever.*
>
> —1 Corinthians 9:24–25 NIV

In what areas of your life would you say you've entered into "strict training." What were the results?

Have you had a teacher, coach, mentor, parent, or another person who poured into you the skills, wisdom, or knowledge they possessed? How did that make you feel? How has the "strict training" in various areas of your life created skills, wisdom, or knowledge that could benefit another? What would it be like for you to pour your life into someone else and cheer them on to win the race?

Lord Jesus, help me understand where I could still benefit from some strict training. Help me realize where I have much to offer others as a leader, parent, coach, or mentor. Help me invest in the right people at the right time and in the right ways. Amen.

Invincible

- Complete the Sherpa Training Session 35: CORE Process: The Intentional Transfer Plan
- Video, 100 Exercise, and X Challenge

Involved

> *Train up a child in the way he should go, and when he is old he will not depart from it.*
>
> —Proverbs 22:6 KJV

One of the things I love about the *Invincible* Sherpa training is how so many concepts are valuable at work and home. Clients frequently share about the positive impact the GiANT tools are having on their families. Please, never use these tools to gain power over another or to manipulate or control anyone. But do use the tools appropriately to train up your children, bless your spouse, lead your team, and impact your community!

Lord Jesus, thank you for these tools that help me understand more about myself, the people around me, and the relational world. Such understanding is vital to living and working in harmony. Help me make the most of this program and use the tools well. Amen.

Invested

A. Please identify your vital insight from this session and write it in your *Breakthrough* Journal.

B. For reflection or discussion:

In this lesson, Jeremie talked about "multiplying your magic" by giving others a chance to learn what you know.

1. What magic do you possess that you can transfer to someone else?
2. How might your skills and wisdom benefit others?
3. What specific ways might you deliver your skills, behaviors, or knowledge to those you lead?

Create your strategy for multiplying your magic:

4. WHAT? Unpack your unconscious competence.
5. TO WHOM? Find the appropriate individuals to transfer your magic.
6. WHEN? Formal/Informal.
7. HOW? Inform, Train, Coach, Apprentice.
8. Name one person at work and the magic you can impart to them.
9. Name one person in your family and the magic you can impart to them.

36

Getting to Clarity with Your Team

Invited

Take my yoke upon you and learn from me, for I am gentle and humble in heart, and you will find rest for your souls. For my yoke is easy and my burden is light.

—Matthew 11:29–30 NIV

Every time I purchase new software designed to make my life easier, I struggle with the steep learning curve. I'm sure the developers see it as easy and light, but they are educated computer professionals who live in a world of geeks. Things that are supposed to be user-friendly seem complicated and frustrating. Why can't things be simple?

In today's session, we look at our plans and ask whether others will easily understand them.

Wouldn't it be great to have a supervisor say their way was easy and the burden was light? What would it take to be this kind of leader for your team? This kind of parent for your teenager? What would it mean to be gentle and humble and model what we hope they will learn?

Rather than merely admiring these words of Jesus, we would do well to model after them. What would it mean to keep issues simple and doable for those you lead? They will thank you for it!

Lord Jesus, in an overly complicated and boggling world, help me to simplify. Let me take on your yoke and learn your gentle and humble ways. Grant me rest for my soul. Make me a leader who keeps matters simple and burdens light for those around me. Amen.

Invincible

- Complete the Sherpa Training Session 36: Getting to Clarity
- Video, 100 Exercise, and X Challenge

Involved

> *You gave your good Spirit to instruct them. You did not withhold your manna from their mouths, and you gave them water for their thirst. For forty years you sustained them in the wilderness; they lacked nothing, their clothes did not wear out nor did their feet become swollen.*
>
> —Nehemiah 9:20–21 NIV

God sustained the Israelites for forty years in the wilderness. They lacked nothing—God provided food, water, clothes, and even healthy feet as they walked! These provisions sustained them on their long journey.

People often understand the energy and resources necessary to initiate something new, but they invariably underestimate what it takes to sustain the project.

What are the provisions your team requires to sustain its productivity and grow?

- Is communication understandable and straightforward?
- Are systems in place to support staff and sustain the momentum or growth?
- Can everyone get on board? What growth barriers can we remove?
- What provisions will be essential to sustain the people and the project?

Lord, as you provided for your people on their long journey, please provide for us today. Reveal what my team requires, so our work is sustainable. Help me provide for those needs. Amen.

Invested

A. Please identify your vital insight from this session and write it in your *Breakthrough* Journal.

B. For reflection or discussion:

1. What does it mean that Jesus's way is easy and his burden light?
2. What would it take to become a leader whose way is easy and the burden light?
3. What would it take to become a spouse or parent whose way is easy and burden light?
4. What does it mean to be gentle and humble of heart?

5. How can you model what you want others to learn and do?
6. Select a current plan or goal. How can you make it simple for others to understand?
7. How might this become scalable and able to grow without breaking?
8. How might this become sustainable and maintained?
9. What would it take to get everyone on board?
10. What is your action item for this session?

37

The Change Equation

Invited

On the third day a wedding took place at Cana in Galilee. Jesus' mother was there, and Jesus and his disciples had also been invited to the wedding. When the wine was gone, Jesus' mother said to him, "They have no more wine."

"Woman, why do you involve me?" Jesus replied. "My hour has not yet come."

His mother said to the servants, "Do whatever he tells you."

Nearby stood six stone water jars, the kind used by the Jews for ceremonial washing, each holding from twenty to thirty gallons.

Jesus said to the servants, "Fill the jars with water"; so they filled them to the brim.

Then he told them, "Now draw some out and take it to the master of the banquet."

They did so, and the master of the banquet tasted the water that had been turned into wine. He did not realize where it had come from, though the servants who had drawn the water knew. Then he called the bridegroom aside and said, "Everyone brings out the choice wine first

> *and then the cheaper wine after the guests have had too much to drink; but you have saved the best till now."*
>
> *What Jesus did here in Cana of Galilee was the first of the signs through which he revealed his glory; and his disciples believed in him.*
>
> —John 2:1–11 NIV

What an incredible example of change! The hosts and guests were about to experience *Dissatisfaction* at the wedding. Running out of wine would ruin the wedding, and people would gossip about this social faux pas for years. Motivated to help her friends, Mary turns to Jesus. Without knowing how, Mary held a *Vision* that Jesus could and would help. Then she laid out the *Natural Next Step* by instructing the servants to do whatever Jesus asked of them. Refusing to accept any hopelessness, Mary cut through the natural inclination of *Resistance* and created the possibility of *Change.*

This story illustrates how dissatisfaction with the status quo, vision for a better future, and the natural next step must be greater than resistance if there will be any change. Today's video session will describe the equation:

Change = D x V x N > Resistance

We could also think of this as faith and hope overcoming fear and helplessness. Jesus rewarded Mary's faith and hope by performing the first recorded miracle of his ministry. He transformed water into wine.

Lord Jesus, use my current dissatisfaction, empowered by a vision for a preferred future, and understanding the natural next step to overcome all my internal resistance. Let me behold your hand transforming my situation and changing my current reality. Let faith and hope overcome my fear and perceived helplessness. I expectantly look for your miraculous change in my life. Amen.

Invincible

- Complete the Sherpa Training Session 37: The Change Equation
- Video, 100 Exercise, and X Challenge

Involved

Where there is no vision, the people perish…

—Proverbs 29:18a KJV

Having a vision of the future is one of the critical components of our change equation. Why?

- Vision clarifies a desired future and provides a destination—an ultimate goal.
- Vision motivates, inspires, and stimulates action.
- Vision provides direction and helps us focus on what matters most.

For the individual, vision answers these three questions:

1. Who do you want to be?
2. For what do you want to be known?
3. What would you like to achieve?

Solomon asserts in Proverbs 29 that without vision from God, people will wander in the dark down a path ultimately leading to destruction. Vision equals God's revelation of truth and reality. Without a compelling vision, there is no change, no improvement, no growth, nor significant accomplishment. Without clear direction, people are doomed to wander in the dark. The light to guide our way comes from vision.

Seeking personal vision asks for God's light and revelation concerning:

- What is my life purpose?
- Why am I on this planet here and now?
- What is God's plan for my life?

Lord Jesus, you are the light of the world. Illuminate your vision for my life. Grant me clarity of purpose. Let vision inspire me to action. Focus my energy on what matters most. Let your ultimate goal for me provide both my motivation and direction. Light the pathway of my life with your truth. Amen.

Invested

A. Please identify your vital insight from this session and write it in your *Breakthrough* Journal.

B. For reflection or discussion:

1. Why is it valuable for us to consider Mary's role in the first recorded miracle of Jesus? What can we learn from her?

2. What is one thing you are dissatisfied with right now?

3. What is the vision for what you would want instead? What do you really, really want?

4. What would be the natural next step to move toward the preferred future?
5. Who do you want to be?
6. For what do you want to be known?
7. What would you like to achieve?
8. What insights do you have about your life purpose?
9. What insights do you have about why you are on this planet here and now?
10. What insights do you have about God's plan for your life?

38

Overcoming Resistance

Invited

> *Everyone who believes that Jesus is the Christ is born of God, and everyone who loves the father loves his child as well. This is how we know that we love the children of God: by loving God and carrying out his commands. In fact, this is love for God: to keep his commands. And his commands are not burdensome, for everyone born of God overcomes the world. This is the victory that has overcome the world, even our faith. Who is it that overcomes the world? Only the one who believes that Jesus is the Son of God.*
>
> —1 John 5:1–5 NIV

You are an overcomer! It may not seem real at times, but that is what God's Word says about you. The one who believes Jesus is the Son of God overcomes the world.

We have discussed how dissatisfaction, vision, and natural next steps must be greater than resistance to create change. Resistance is often a looming and intimidating reality to overcome.

- Immovable barriers may require pursuing another direction.
- Avoiding hurdles will take effort, energy, and coordination.
- There may be gaps in the pathway to fill before moving forward becomes possible.

Fear not, do not despair, and never give up. The power of Christ in you is sufficient to overcome the barriers, hurdles, and gaps of resistance. Engage your faith to overcome!

Merciful God, your grace is beyond measure. Let me know your power and grace to overcome the obstacles in my life. Let the things standing in my way become examples of your limitless power. Clothe me with strength as I live my life in your righteous name. I know that in Christ, I am an overcomer. Empower me to overcome the resistance often blocking my way. Show me today how to overcome the barrier, hurdle, or gap hindering my progress. Let me walk forth in the victory Christ has won. Thank you. Amen.

Invincible

- Complete the Sherpa Training Session 38: Overcoming Resistance
- Video, 100 Exercise, and X Challenge

Involved

> *I have told you these things, so that in me you may have peace. In this world you will have trouble. But take heart! I have overcome the world.*
>
> —John 16:33 NIV

Every life has some trouble. The human reality on planet Earth includes pleasure and pain, joy and sorrow, happiness and sadness, ease and difficulty, as well as blessings and trouble. Jesus forewarns us about this so that we might have peace even during challenges.

In a world full of trouble, we can take heart because Christ has overcome the world. He promises to always be with us in the midst of the challenges of life. Taking heart involves shifting focus *from* our frustration regarding the obstacles in our way and *toward* the victory Christ has won. Turning our attention from trouble to Christ makes all the difference! Keeping our gaze upon Christ provides peace.

O Lord my God, your power endures throughout all generations. In the difficulties I face, let me know you go before me and fight for me. Let me rest in you while you fight my battles. Like David conquered Goliath, I call on you to defeat the giant obstacles in my life. You are the solid foundation on which I build my life, make me secure through the storms that will come. Break down any obstacle standing in the path you have planned for me. Let me trust you are directing my steps and your strength is all I need. Amen.

Invested

A. Please identify your vital insight from this session and write it in your *Breakthrough* Journal.

B. For reflection or discussion:

1. What specific change do you desire, or what project do you want to complete?
2. What immovable barriers are in your way?

3. What new directions might you pursue to sidestep these barriers?
4. What are the hurdles in your way?
5. What would it take to jump over them?
6. What gaps might need to be filled?
7. Who or what might assist in filling those gaps?
8. How might you change your gaze from your trouble toward the victory of Jesus?
9. What steps would help you overcome current trouble?
10. What does it mean that Christ is always with you in the midst of the challenges of life? When have you experienced this in the past? In what situation do you need to remember this now?

39

Getting Others to the Next Level

Invited

> *As Jesus was walking beside the Sea of Galilee, he saw two brothers, Simon called Peter and his brother Andrew. They were casting a net into the lake, for they were fishermen. "Come, follow me," Jesus said, "and I will send you out to fish for people." At once they left their nets and followed him.*
>
> *Going on from there, he saw two other brothers, James son of Zebedee and his brother John. They were in a boat with their father Zebedee, preparing their nets. Jesus called them, and immediately they left the boat and their father and followed him.*
>
> —Matthew 4:18–22 NIV

Jesus chose specific men to follow him. They had no idea what might happen or where answering this call would lead them. We might wonder why men would leave their work and take off down the road following another man. They must have sensed a possibility that would lift them above the typical day-to-day drudgery. Perhaps they thought following Jesus would boost their life to another whole dimension—and it did!

What about those you lead?

- Do you have a way to measure the level their current performance is on?
- Do you have a goal of raising them to the next level?
- Do they know you are calling them to something greater?
- Do they know you believe in their potential?
- Do they know you are committed to calibrating support and challenge that you may empower their climb to greater heights?

Lord Jesus, help me choose my team wisely. Let me assess their potential clearly and discern their path to the next level. I want my team to succeed. May I incorporate the tools we have been learning to lead my team well. Amen.

Invincible

- Complete the Sherpa Training Session 39: Getting Others to the Next Level.
- Video, 100 Exercise, and X Challenge

Involved

For the Spirit God gave us does not make us timid, but gives us power, love and self-discipline.

—2 Timothy 1:7 NIV

A timid person will likely not become a successful leader. The dictionary definition of timid describes one lacking courage or confidence or one who is easily frightened. Synonyms for timid include cautious, uncertain, reticent, and insecure. Timidity is not something to list on your resume.

Yet, many in leadership positions are timid about influencing their charges to grow and attain the next level. Some dominant leaders will not invest in their protégé's development out of concern that a talented younger person might replace them. Protectors may be reticent to challenge others. Certainly, abdicators have never created the goals, priorities, or systems that promote growth. The best leaders are liberators, creating opportunities and empowering their followers to reach the next level.

What are the needs of the people we lead?

- to understand what to do
- a clear path forward
- genuine assistance
- support and challenge

We can lead well because God never intended us to be timid. The Spirit of God gives us power, love, and self-discipline. These three remarkable qualities allow us to lead with conviction and clarity.

- God gives us energy and strength to define and navigate the path upward.
- God gives us love to fight for the highest possible good in the lives of those we lead.
- God gives us self-discipline to honestly evaluate others and to call them up!

God, take from me any drop of timidity that would try to steal my effectiveness as a leader. Give me the power to accomplish all you put before me. Let your love flowing through me call others up to the next level. Give me the self-discipline to walk with them and see them grow and conquer the mountain. Amen.

Invested

A. Please identify your vital insight from this session and write it in your *Breakthrough* Journal.

B. For reflection or discussion:

Think about one person you lead or influence and answer the following:

1. At what level is this person functioning? Are they meeting expectations for that level?
2. What is the next level up their path? Do they have the potential to make it?
3. What are the expectations of the next level? Where should they improve to fulfill these expectations?
4. How might you and your team recognize you have "called" your team to follow you?
5. At times, you may feel you get "stuck" with your team. What ought to change in your mind or in your team to create a healthier reality?
6. Where might timidity have kept you from being all God wants you to be?
7. What might improve if you demonstrate God has given you a spirit of power?

8. How will you reveal God's love for your team and fight for their highest possible good?
9. In what situation should you claim the self-discipline God has provided?

40

The Two Sides of Leadership

Invited

> *They were on their way up to Jerusalem, with Jesus leading the way...*
>
> —Mark 10: 32a NIV

Intentionality was critical to the ministry of Jesus. His leading had two concurrent outcomes. Jesus walked the way that revealed who he was and the purpose for which he came. At the same time, he transformed the lives of his disciples. Think of these two functions of Jesus's ministry as parallel rails like a train track.

The traditional railway trains have served as transportation since the nineteenth century ran on two rails. Both rails must be present, and they must be parallel. Otherwise, the train will grind to a screeching halt.

It's interesting how the mission of Jesus also ran on two rails. First and foremost was the saving work of his suffering, death, and resurrection to take away the sins of the world. Secondly, it was necessary to train a band of people who would spread the message of God's love and salvation after he was gone.

Jesus accomplished both his primary purpose and preparation of others to fulfill their purpose. So, too, he has with us. We each have our primary tasks to perform at work or home, and we each have the responsibility to develop others along the way. Building others up, helping them grow, and encouraging them to the next level is the second rail of leadership. Leadership is merely being a person of influence in whatever area God has planted you.

Lord, grant me an awareness of both rails that my life runs on. On one rail, you are working in me and empowering me to be a productive human. On the other rail, you challenge me to invest in others along the way. May I be blessed to be a blessing. Let my actions demonstrate love for God and others. Amen.

Invincible

- Complete the Sherpa Training Session 40: The Two Sides of Leadership
- Video, 100 Exercise, and X Challenge

Involved

> *Therefore go and make disciples of all nations, baptizing them in the name of the Father and of the Son and of the Holy Spirit, and teaching them to obey everything I have commanded you.*
>
> —Matt 28: 19–20a NIV

Some professions focus explicitly on the equipping of others. Teachers, pastors, counselors, coaches, and many others focus their lives to help others learn, grow, and become more competent. But in many other professions, teaching others becomes a secondary and too often forgotten function.

Many a sermon preached on this passage mentions the wording at the beginning. "Go and make disciples…" is not only about sending missionaries to distant lands to preach the gospel. When we look at the original language, it might better be interpreted with the words, "As you are going, make disciples…"

- As you are going about your daily activities - disciple your children, family, and friends.
- As you are working, disciple those around you and those you lead.

One of the reasons I love this Sherpa training is because it is like "discipling without the Bible verses." These principles promote Christ-like attitudes, speech, and actions. You are transformed as you treat others well. You make a difference in a person's life when you fight for their highest possible good. You impact a life when you calibrate both support and challenge in a way that empowers them.

The Two Sides Of Leadership tool reminds us to invest in those around us and their success in the same way we invest in our success. As so many coaches have said, "There is no 'I' in team." Should you improve your skills and be productive with your time? Absolutely! At the same time, be intentional about investing in those around you. Use these visual tools and additional resources to teach others a better and more productive way of living.

Lord, I want to be productive in life, in my work, and for your Kingdom. I choose each day to be your disciple. But discipleship is not an individual activity. Discipleship involves relationships and community. Help me identify those you call me to disciple as I am going along life's path. Empower me to live in such a way that they will see Jesus in how I treat them. Help me be intentional about teaching them Sherpa tools that will improve their lives and this world. Amen.

Invested

A. Please identify your vital insight from this session and write it in your *Breakthrough* Journal.

B. For reflection or discussion:

1. What might have happened if Jesus simply attended to his primary purpose of dying for the sins of the world without discipling a group of people to share the news?
2. What aspects of your work (or life) lend themselves to apprenticing others and sharing your expertise with them?
3. In what ways might you define your success according to how well you lead those around you? (Remember, sometimes we lead from the middle, not just from the top.)
4. Describe how your life runs on two rails. At work. At home. In the community.
5. How can you demonstrate the presence of Jesus in your workplace? In your home? In the community?
6. How might you disciple others without quoting Bible verses?
7. Without ever being named, how might Jesus impact others through you?

8. For which of your responsibilities would you like to improve your performance?
9. What is your action plan for growth in these areas?

41

CORE Process: Intentional Transfer Plan

Invited

> *For this reason we also, from the day we heard about you, have not ceased praying for you and asking God to fill you with the knowledge of his will in all spiritual wisdom and understanding, so that you may live worthily of the Lord and please him in all respects—bearing fruit in every good deed, growing in the knowledge of God, being strengthened with all power according to his glorious might for the display of all patience and steadfastness, joyfully giving thanks to the Father who has qualified you to share in the saints' inheritance in the light. He delivered us from the power of darkness and transferred us to the kingdom of the Son he loves, in whom we have redemption, the forgiveness of sins.*
>
> —Colossians 1:9–14 NET

God transferred us in a big way! We have been delivered from the power of darkness and transferred to the kingdom of light through Jesus Christ. This deliverance is not our doing. You and I did nothing to earn or deserve God's love and mercy. Jesus did it all. This transfer happened totally because of the redemption won for us by the death and resurrection of Jesus. So what ought we to do? A 500-year-old Christian saying puts it this way.

> *Pray as though everything depended on God;*
> *Act as though everything depended on you.*

For today's lesson, I would like to change this a bit:

> *Know that redemption's transfer is all because of Jesus,*
> *Invest your life in serving others as if it were all up to you.*

Faith will naturally bear fruit. The fruit we focus on today is the intentional transfer of our abilities, understanding, and expertise to our family or our team. It's our responsibility to invest in them and assist them in becoming all God wants them to be.

Lord Jesus, help me understand what you want me to do. Make me wise about spiritual things. May the way I live always please and honor you. Fill me with your mighty, glorious strength so I can keep going no matter what happens—full of the joy of the Lord. May I come to know God better by doing good and kind things for others. Thank you for giving me the skills, knowledge, and expertise you now call me to transfer to others. Please give me your direction and plan for developing those you have put into my life. Amen.

Invincible

- Complete the Sherpa Training Session 41: Intentional Transfer Plan
- Video, 100 Exercise, and X Challenge

Involved

> *Jesus went through all the towns and villages, teaching in their synagogues, proclaiming the good news of the kingdom and healing every disease and sickness. When he saw the crowds, he had compassion on them, because they were harassed and helpless, like sheep without a shepherd. Then he said to his disciples, "The harvest is plentiful but the workers are few. Ask the Lord of the harvest, therefore, to send out workers into his harvest field."*
>
> —Matthew 9:35–38 NIV

Never pray a prayer unless you are willing for God to use you as the answer. Are you willing to work in the field? Are you willing to raise up the additional workers? Start with *one.*

The leader doesn't pass the buck.

- If workers are required, what might you do to recruit and equip them?
- If people need to reach the next level, what are you doing as Sherpa to empower their climb?
- If you can't do it all yourself, what are you doing to apprentice others so they can carry part of your load?

Investing in those around you is your God-given responsibility.

Lord, there is work to be done. It seems too often the laborers are few. Help me build my team to make a difference in your world. Teach me to be a harvester and send me into your fields. Amen.

Invested

A. Please identify your vital insight from this session and write it in your *Breakthrough* Journal.

B. For reflection or discussion:

1. What are your thoughts about this old saying?

   Pray as though everything depended on God;
   Act as though everything depended on you.

2. How can you demonstrate at work that God has *delivered you from the power of darkness and transferred you to the kingdom of the Son*?

3. If workers are required, what might you do to recruit and equip them?

4. If people need to reach the next level, what are you doing as Sherpa to empower their climb?

5. If you can't do it all yourself, what are you doing to apprentice others so they can carry part of your load?

6. What valuable understanding did you gain from each of these ten topics? Which ones are most pertinent to your current situation?

   a. Multiplying Magic
   b. The Developing Others Tool
   c. The Responsive Leader Tool
   d. The Investing Time Tool
   e. The Expectations Scale Tool
   f. The Clarity Tool
   g. The Change Equation Tool
   h. Overcoming Resistance
   i. Getting Others to the Next Level
   j. The Two Sides of Leadership

42

Maximizing Performance

How to Lead Organizations Worth Following

Invited

> *Make a tree good and its fruit will be good, or make a tree bad and its fruit will be bad, for a tree is recognized by its fruit.*
>
> —Matthew 12:33 NIV

Let's rephrase this verse. Make an organization's culture good, and the results will be good. Make an organizational culture bad, and the results will be bad. Every organization is known by the results it produces.

This concept goes far beyond simply whether they can make a useful widget or a profit at the end of the year. God measures fruit according to its effect on the lives of the employees, the customers, the community, and creation. Making money at all costs is not bearing good fruit. Damaging individuals, harming God's creation, and promoting unhealthy goods or activities is rotten fruit.

If we want an organization worth joining and supporting, it will require evaluating our motives, methods, and results on multiple levels.

Lord, reveal your definition of good fruit—your definition of success. Uncover those hidden things that may poison our tree. Help us work with you toward creating a healthy culture at home, at work, and in the community. We want to bear fruit you will view and say, "It is most certainly good!" Amen.

Invincible

- Complete the Sherpa Training Session 42: Maximizing Performance
- Video, 100 Exercise, and X Challenge

Involved

> *Jesus knew their thoughts and said to them, "Every kingdom divided against itself will be ruined, and every city or household divided against itself will not stand.*
>
> —Matthew 12:25 NIV

A team without unity and connectedness will not stand. It will not produce anywhere near its potential. Organizations can invest all the time and money they want to gain traction, but you won't get far without trust in the relationships.

Trust comes before traction!

Too many organizations want to focus on moving forward by creating alignment, improving execution, and increasing capacity. They are building on sand without the foundation of trust.

Trust comes by investing attention toward improving communication and building healthy relationships. Here is where the 5 Voices are vital. We start with Know Yourself to Lead Yourself and then move on to Know your Team to Lead your Team. Nearly half of the sixty GiANT visual tools enhance Communication and Relationships. They all work together to combat division and promote a healthy organizational culture.

One of the most critical aspects of leadership is to build trust. What can you do as a leader to improve communication and strengthen relationships at home, on your team, in your organization, in your community?

God, if my team members can't trust each other, we are in big trouble. Please help us identify those things that might divide us. Help us to speak clearly and listen well. Let us invest in our relationships so we might be more unified, efficient, and productive. Help me to be a humble servant-leader who calibrates support and challenge well in every relationship. Amen.

Invested

A. Please identify your vital insight from this session and write it in your *Breakthrough* Journal.

B. For reflection or discussion:

1. What communication tendencies in your workplace are unhelpful or unhealthy?
2. What communication tendencies in your workplace are helpful or healthy?

3. What relationship tendencies in your workplace are unhelpful or unhealthy?
4. What relationship tendencies in your workplace are helpful or healthy?
5. What tendencies in your workplace work against healthy alignment?
6. What tendencies in your workplace work toward healthy alignment?
7. What tendencies in your workplace limit execution?
8. What tendencies in your workplace foster execution?
9. What tendencies in your workplace limit capacity?
10. What tendencies in your workplace increase capacity?

43

Go to the Source

How to Defeat Drama and Gossip

Invited

> *If a fellow believer hurts you, go and tell him—work it out between the two of you. If he listens, you've made a friend. If he won't listen, take one or two others along so that the presence of witnesses will keep things honest, and try again. If he still won't listen, tell the church. If he won't listen to the church, you'll have to start over from scratch, confront him with the need for repentance, and offer again God's forgiving love.*
>
> —Matthew 18:15–17 MSG

Workplace drama and gossip can lead to absenteeism, turnover, and lawsuits. Ignoring, avoiding, or denying drama only increases its power. Drama manifests in various ways in the workplace: insubordination, backstabbing, petty arguments, power struggles, and all manner of employee-relationship issues.

Those who create workplace drama aren't always doing it intentionally. Sometimes their behavior is driven by insecurity, fear, or other undealt-with emotional issues. But in most cases, I believe drama stems from people not knowing how to handle conflict.

Jesus gives us a formula for handling conflict in Matthew 18. His words are direct and straightforward. If someone has hurt you, go and tell them. Unfortunately, people are usually tempted to go and tell others behind the person's back. We all like to gather people on "our side" of an issue. It is far more comfortable and enjoyable to talk *about* the problem person than talk *to* them. But Jesus clearly instructs us "go, talk to them, and work it out between the two of you." If that doesn't work, step two is taking an unbiased facilitator with you and trying again. Jesus provides steps beyond this, too. (Please re-read the above Bible passage.)

Some people may challenge that the church and the workplace are not equal entities. But being a pastor for over 20 years, I will guarantee you that most any difficulty occurring in a workplace has also happened in a church. The bottom line is this: drama and gossip are damaging to people and productivity. The Go to the Source tool is effective in reducing drama and gossip as much as possible.

Lord Jesus, I confess there have been times I talked about people instead of going to them and working out our differences or difficulties. Forgive me. Let me follow your plan that helps eliminate drama and gossip in my circles of influence. Grant me the courage to speak up and work out problems face to face. Let your forgiving love flow through me to the offenders in my life. Amen.

Invincible

- Complete the Sherpa Training Session 43: How to Defeat Drama and Gossip
- Video, 100 Exercise, and X Challenge

Involved

A gossip betrays a confidence;
so avoid anyone who talks too much.

—Proverbs 20:19 NIV

A scoundrel plots evil,
and on their lips it is like a scorching fire.
A perverse person stirs up conflict,
and a gossip separates close friends.
A violent person entices their neighbor
and leads them down a path that is not good.

—Proverbs 16:27–29 NIV

Without wood a fire goes out;
without a gossip a quarrel dies down.
As charcoal to embers and as wood to fire,
so is a quarrelsome person for kindling strife.
The words of a gossip are like choice morsels;
they go down to the inmost parts.

—Proverbs 26:20–22 NIV

Gossip leads to toxicity. It creates a culture of fear and mistrust and makes everyone less happy at work. The person who is the subject of the talk feels ridiculed and embarrassed, and everyone else realizes they have to watch their backs. None of this allows for creativity, efficiency, or positivity in the workplace.

Workplace gossip is a form of informal communication among colleagues focused on others' private, personal, and sensitive affairs. Businesses that don't have proactive policies in place to combat gossiping may find themselves in a weaker position should an associated case come to a hearing.

The root cause of gossip is almost always jealousy. The more successful, attractive, kind, or self-assured you are, the more people will be tempted to gossip. It is an attempt to bring you down. It is also an attempt to bring themselves up in comparison. But the toxicity of gossip generates a high price to pay.

Some organizations using the Go to the Source tool have declared their workplace a "gossip-free zone!" It's a great idea to preemptively talk about the problem to create a pathway toward a healthier organizational culture.

Lord Jesus, keep my lips from spreading gossip or drama. Instead, let my words be pure, truthful, and full of quiet gentleness. Let my speech be positive, courteous, and full of mercy. May I become a peacemaker, planting seeds of peace and reaping a harvest of goodness and righteousness. Amen.

Invested

A. Please identify your vital insight from this session and write it in your *Breakthrough* Journal.

B. For reflection or discussion:

1. When did your words of drama or gossip harm someone else or get you into trouble?
2. When did someone else's gossip or drama harm you?
3. Why is Go to the Source such a crucial value for building healthy teams?
4. When have you displayed conduit tendencies?
5. When have you demonstrated firewall tendencies?
6. What does building a firewall mean to you?
7. How might you help create a firewall culture at your workplace?
8. What situation would be improved if you go to the source and work out an issue?
9. Describe a time you used Matthew 18 to settle an issue or when you witnessed someone else use this pattern.
10. What is your action item for this session?

44

Using Discretion and Discipline

Invited

Whoever loves discipline loves knowledge,
but whoever hates correction is stupid. …
The way of fools seems right to them,
but the wise listen to advice.
Fools show their annoyance at once,
but the prudent overlook an insult. …
The words of the reckless pierce like swords,
but the tongue of the wise brings healing. …
The prudent keep their knowledge to themselves,
but a fool's heart blurts out folly.

—Proverbs 12:1, 15, 16, 18, 23 NIV

Have you ever said the right thing but to the wrong person, in the wrong way, or at the wrong time? The results likely ranged from poor to disastrous even when you believed you were in the right. Lack of discretion and discipline in communication can cause significant difficulties.

The next tool encourages us to think before we speak and ask ourselves three questions:

1. What should I share?
2. With whom should I share it?
3. When should I share it?

Discretion and discipline can keep us from making foolish mistakes and improve our interactions at home, at work, and beyond.

Lord Jesus, I want to love discipline and knowledge, listen to advice, and welcome correction. Help me overlook insults and hold my tongue when required. Keep me from blurting out folly, and let my words deliver wisdom and healing. Amen.

Invincible

- Complete the Sherpa Training Session 44: Discretion and Discipline
- Video, 100 Exercise, and X Challenge

Involved

... pay attention to my wisdom,
turn your ear to my words of insight,
that you may maintain discretion
and your lips may preserve knowledge.

—Proverbs 5:1–2 NIV

Then you will understand what is right and just
and fair—every good path.
For wisdom will enter your heart,
and knowledge will be pleasant to your soul.
Discretion will protect you,
and understanding will guard you.

—Proverbs 2:9–11 NIV

... do not let wisdom and understanding out of your sight,
preserve sound judgment and discretion;
they will be life for you,
an ornament to grace your neck.

—Proverbs 3:21–22 NIV

Discretion is the quality of behaving or speaking in such a way as to avoid causing offense or revealing private information. Discretion avoids attracting attention and keeps confidential what ought to be held close. Discretion also prevents careless speech or offensive words.

An example of discretion is avoiding talking about politics at family dinners, especially if you know someone in the room supported the other candidate!

This 2,500-year-old proverb instructs that maintaining discretion will protect you. It declares sound judgment and discretion will be life for you and protect you. Discretion sounds pretty valuable!

Lord Jesus, may my lips maintain discretion and preserve knowledge. May I understand what is right, just, and honest. May wisdom enter my heart, and understanding guard my ways. Let sound judgment and discretion adorn my life. Amen.

Invested

A. Please identify your vital insight from this session and write it in your *Breakthrough* Journal.

B. For reflection or discussion:

1. Share an example of when saying the wrong thing at the wrong time created unnecessary drama or conflict.
2. If the Discretion and Discipline tool were used, how might the situation have been handled differently?
3. In the future, what guidelines might you use to discern *what* to share and how much?
4. What guidelines might you use to discern *who* to share with and whether they are the right people?
5. What guidelines might you use to discern *when* to share and whether now is the right time?
6. How might using discretion and discipline address typical "tone and tact" mistakes many people make?
7. How might using discretion and discipline reduce confusion and enhance clarity?
8. How does a lack of discretion and discipline undermine one's authority and credibility?

9. What are your tendencies? A) Do you tend to share the wrong things? B) Do you share with the wrong people? C) Do you share too early, or perhaps too late?

10. What is your action item from this session?

45

Communicating Clearly with Provisional Plan Promise

Invited

> *"Though I have been speaking figuratively, a time is coming when I will no longer use this kind of language but will tell you plainly about my Father. In that day you will ask in my name. I am not saying that I will ask the Father on your behalf. No, the Father himself loves you because you have loved me and have believed that I came from God. I came from the Father and entered the world; now I am leaving the world and going back to the Father." Then Jesus' disciples said, "Now you are speaking clearly and without figures of speech. Now we can see that you know all things and that you do not even need to have anyone ask you questions. This makes us believe that you came from God."*
>
> —John 16: 25–30 NIV

Jesus taught using stories and parables that often left the listener to discern the meaning. Even those closest to him didn't comprehend the full implications of his role and his mission. As his time was drawing near, Jesus declared he would no longer speak figuratively but would tell them plainly and directly.

Our high-pressure, fast-paced, and exacting business world is no place for ambiguous language that leaves people guessing the meaning. It is necessary to speak plainly and leave others fully understanding with no doubts. People want to know where things are going and what the expectations are.

Using the Provisional Plan Promise tool will prevent misunderstandings and help keep the whole team on the same page.

Lord Jesus, you clearly communicated who you were, why you came from heaven, and what your mission accomplished on this earth. Help me clearly communicate so my team will understand our direction, mission, and the tasks to complete. Amen.

Invincible

- Complete the Sherpa Training Session 45: Provisional Plan Promise
- Video, 100 Exercise, and X Challenge

Involved

"Therefore let all Israel be assured of this: God has made this Jesus, whom you crucified, both Lord and Messiah." When the people heard this, they were cut to the heart and said to Peter and the other apostles, "Brothers, what shall we do?" Peter replied, "Repent and be baptized, every one of you, in the name of Jesus Christ for the forgiveness of your sins. And you will receive the gift of the Holy Spirit. The promise is for you and your children and for all who are far off—for all whom the Lord our God will call."

—Acts 2: 36–39 NIV

"Repent, be baptized, and you will receive the gift of the Holy Spirit." Peter is not brainstorming or using possibility thinking. Peter is not setting a direction that might change as new information arose. Peter is declaring a promise of what God does and will do for future generations until Jesus returns.

You can stand on a rock-solid promise. Come hell or high water, a promise must be kept. Therefore, we ought never to make promises unless we are sure we will keep them.

Too many spouses and children have been hurt when someone made a promise and didn't keep it. It was often a misunderstanding—they were merely verbalizing possibilities, and it sounded like a promise. Perhaps they had a plan but didn't realize it would need to adjust as more information arose. They should never have made a promise, or they should never have let their audience interpret it as a promise.

But when God makes a promise, you can rest assured it will happen. Chaplain Adele M. Gill wrote of Seven Promises of God.

God Promises:

1. I will be with you.
2. I will protect you.
3. I will be your strength.
4. I will answer you.
5. I will provide for you.
6. I will give you peace.
7. I will always love you.

These promises are an excellent start, and of course, we will add to them the promise of the Holy Spirit that Peter declared in Acts chapter 2.

What about you? Would people declare you are a person who keeps their promises? Or have you been sloppy about communicating whether your words are Provisional, Plan, or Promise?

Loving God, thank you for your promises. Let me claim and hold onto the fact *you are with me, you protect me, you are my strength, you answer prayer, you provide for me, you give me peace, and you always love me. Thank you for the promised Holy Spirit's presence always with and within me. You keep your promises. Help me keep mine. Amen.*

Invested

A. Please identify your vital insight from this session and write it in your *Breakthrough* Journal.

B. For reflection or discussion:

1. When might you (or someone you know) have verbalized possibilities and the hearers misconstrued it as a plan or promise?
2. When it comes to Provisional Plan Promise, what are your default tendencies?
3. Do you think out loud about possibilities, or are you more of a planner?
4. How can this tool help teams stay focused, productive, and on the same page?
5. Why is it important to communicate the relative certainty of ideas or initiatives?
6. Which promises from God are easy for you to believe and receive?
7. Which promises from God are more elusive for you?
8. What might help you communicate with more clarity with your family or team?
9. What is your action item for this session?

46

The Power of the Medium

Invited

> *Therefore see that you walk carefully [living life with honor, purpose, and courage; shunning those who tolerate and enable evil], not as the unwise, but as wise [sensible, intelligent, discerning people], making the very most of your time [on earth, recognizing and taking advantage of each opportunity and using it with wisdom and diligence]...*
>
> —Ephesians 5:15–16a AMP

Today, let's put this verse together with four of our foundational Sherpa principles.

- *See that you walk carefully* as you intentionally influence self, family, team, organization, and community. (5 Circles of Influence)
- *Live with honor, purpose, and courage* as you calibrate support and challenge to empower and liberate others. (Support Challenge Matrix)

- *As wise, sensible, intelligent, discerning people,* fight for the highest possible good in the lives of those you lead. (Liberating Others)
- *Take advantage of each opportunity and use it with wisdom and diligence* as you draw out and utilize the gifts and strengths of the Nurturers, Creatives, Guardians, Connectors, and Pioneers around you. (5 Voices)

Lord, as I attempt all these challenges, please help me think intentionally about the person on the other side of me, the message I want to communicate, and the best way to do it. Amen.

Invincible

- Complete the Sherpa Training Session 46: Effective Delegation
- Video, 100 Exercise, and X Challenge

Involved

> *For the time will come when people will not tolerate sound doctrine and accurate instruction [that challenges them with God's truth]; but wanting to have their ears tickled [with something pleasing], they will accumulate for themselves [many] teachers [one after another, chosen] to satisfy their own desires and to support the errors they hold, and will turn their ears away from the truth and will wander off into myths and man-made fictions [and will accept the unacceptable].*
>
> —2 Timothy 4:3–4 AMP

Challenge is important. Challenge is necessary. Challenge is crucial. Throughout the old testament, when God's people strayed, the Lord sent a prophet to reveal the truth. There are times when the church, society, politics, business, and many other aspects of culture deserve a good old-fashioned prophetic challenge.

In your circles of influence, who is God calling you to challenge? What is the prophetic message that will help another person get back on course? What is the most effective medium for you to use when you bring that challenge?

Remember: if we say the "right" thing in the "wrong" way, it can do more harm than good. Nonetheless, we must calibrate *both* support and challenge. There are tremendous benefits when we learn to give a challenge effectively.

Dear Lord, let me communicate challenge combining grace and prophetic zeal. Without being challenged, people wander off into false narratives and accept the unacceptable. That has to stop. Amen.

Invested

A. Please identify your vital insight from this session and write it in your *Breakthrough* Journal.

B. For reflection or discussion:

1. Over the last month, when you brought challenges, what medium did you use? Was it appropriate?
2. Where might it be helpful for you to shift into reverse and apologize?
3. What medium do you tend to overuse? What medium might you avoid? How is that working for you?

4. What is the culture of your team when it comes to challenges?
5. Does your team use the right medium in the right situation?
6. How would your team culture improve if you built this little tool into your values?
7. Share an example of when challenging someone using the wrong medium created problems. What should have happened?
8. What is your action item for this session?

47

Effective Delegation

Invited

A few days later, when Jesus again entered Capernaum, the people heard that he had come home. They gathered in such large numbers that there was no room left, not even outside the door, and he preached the word to them. Some men came, bringing to him a paralyzed man, carried by four of them. Since they could not get him to Jesus because of the crowd, they made an opening in the roof above Jesus by digging through it and then lowered the mat the man was lying on. When Jesus saw their faith, he said to the paralyzed man, "Son, your sins are forgiven."

Now some teachers of the law were sitting there, thinking to themselves, "Why does this fellow talk like that? He's blaspheming! Who can forgive sins but God alone?"

Immediately Jesus knew in his spirit that this was what they were thinking in their hearts, and he said to them, "Why are you thinking these things? Which is easier: to say to this paralyzed man, 'Your sins are forgiven,' or to say, 'Get up, take your mat and walk'? But I want you to know that the Son of Man has authority on earth to forgive sins." So he said to the man, "I tell you, get up, take your mat and go home." He got up, took his

> *mat and walked out in full view of them all. This amazed everyone and they praised God, saying, "We have never seen anything like this!"*
>
> —Mark 2:1–12 NIV

Jesus carried a responsibility more extraordinary than anyone else who ever walked on this earth. The responsibility to remain absolutely attuned to almighty God as well as the responsibility to bear the sins of humanity and reconcile sinful humans with a perfect God.

Jesus shocked the religious leaders of the day by announcing the forgiveness of sins. Then he demonstrated his power by healing the paralyzed man. The crowd was amazed because they had "never seen anything like this."

God not only assigned Jesus responsibilities to accomplish but gave him the power and authority to match the responsibility. One without the other creates imbalance and difficulties (even impossibilities) for the individual and those around him.

We would do well to make sure that responsibility and authority are balanced. Without commensurate authority, many responsibilities become either unrealistic or impossible.

Jesus Christ, I give you thanks and praise, for you have both the authority to heal the human soul (forgive sins) and the authority to heal the human body. Blessed are you, my Savior and my Lord. Amen.

Invincible

- Complete the Sherpa Training Session 47: Effective Delegation
- Video, 100 Exercise, and X Challenge

Involved

All this happened to King Nebuchadnezzar. Twelve months later, as the king was walking on the roof of the royal palace of Babylon, he said, "Is not this the great Babylon I have built as the royal residence, by my mighty power and for the glory of my majesty?"

Even as the words were on his lips, a voice came from heaven, "This is what is decreed for you, King Nebuchadnezzar: Your royal authority has been taken from you. You will be driven away from people and will live with the wild animals; you will eat grass like the ox. Seven times will pass by for you until you acknowledge that the Most High is sovereign over all kingdoms on earth and gives them to anyone he wishes."

—Daniel 4:28–32 NIV

Kings have absolute authority over their subjects. They make all the rules and are not accountable to anyone—or so it seems. But great King Nebuchadnezzar of Babylon found out differently. He found out a "King of Kings and Lord of Lords" has power and authority that exceeded his own. Nebuchadnezzar's authority, power, wealth, and much more were all taken away until he would acknowledge the Most High is sovereign over all kingdoms of the earth.

Whether you wield great authority or hardly any; whether you have wealth or struggle financially; whether you lead multitudes or a few—let us all take our place as humble servants to the Most High God. Let God be King and Authority over your heart, mind, speech, actions, family, relationships, work, business dealings, and every aspect of your life.

Blessed are you, Lord our God, King of the Universe, who created the heavens and the earth. We acknowledge your authority, and we happily and humbly take our place as your subjects. Rule and reign over us. Provide for us and protect us. And grant us to reflect your goodness by using well the authority assigned to us in our lives. Amen.

Invested

A. Please identify your vital insight from this session and write it in your *Breakthrough* Journal.

B. For reflection or discussion:

1. What are your tendencies when delegating responsibility and authority?
2. In what kinds of situations might you be tempted toward self-preservation?
3. In what kinds of situations might you be tempted to disempower others?
4. What did you learn about yourself when you saw the Effective Delegation tool?
5. Give an example of when you empowered another by delegating both authority and responsibility in appropriate measure.
6. Describe the sources and consequences of unhealthy delegation.
7. How might you use this tool to expand the capacity or improve the execution of your team?
8. How might you better empower others to create a high-performing team?

9. What kinds of responsibility and authority has Jesus delegated to you?
10. How might your use of responsibility and authority demonstrate the Lordship of Christ in your life?

48

Push/Pull Leadership and Coaching Skills

Invited

> *You have heard that it was said to the people long ago, 'You shall not murder, and anyone who murders will be subject to judgment.' But I tell you that anyone who is angry with a brother or sister will be subject to judgment. …*
>
> *You have heard that it was said, 'Eye for eye, and tooth for tooth.' But I tell you, do not resist an evil person. If anyone slaps you on the right cheek, turn to them the other cheek also. And if anyone wants to sue you and take your shirt, hand over your coat as well. If anyone forces you to go one mile, go with them two miles. Give to the one who asks you, and do not turn away from the one who wants to borrow from you. …*
>
> *You have heard that it was said, 'Love your neighbor and hate your enemy.' But I tell you, love your enemies and pray for those who persecute you, that you may be children of your Father in heaven. He causes his sun to rise on the evil and the good, and sends rain on the righteous and the unrighteous.*
>
> —Matthew 5:21–22a, 38–42, 43–45 NIV

"You have heard, but I tell you" is a pattern Jesus used when challenging the status quo and establishing new standards. The new directives Jesus gives his followers are never more comfortable than their current situation. Jesus makes living for God even harder.

- Anyone who is angry is subject to judgment.
- Turn the other cheek, and go a second mile.
- Love your enemies, and pray for those who persecute you.

Jesus was never afraid to give his views and opinions or declare what God wanted people to do, even when it would seem difficult or unpopular to the listeners. Jesus did "push" and challenge people. He would boldly tell it like it is.

Lord Jesus, show me when and how to be straightforward when communicating with others. Let me no longer be inhibited by what they might think of me. Let my words exemplify the paradox of speaking the truth in love. Amen.

Invincible

- Complete the Sherpa Training Session 48: Push/Pull
- Video, 100 Exercise, and X Challenge

Involved

> *Ask and it will be given to you; seek and you will find; knock and the door will be opened to you. For everyone who asks receives; the one who seeks finds; and to the one who knocks, the door will be opened.*
>
> —Matthew 7:7–8 NIV

Open and honest communication through which everyone's viewpoint can be heard and considered is necessary for people to work together successfully. The best way to find out what is going on in another person's mind is by asking non-threatening open-ended questions. Seek the gift and insight each person brings to the table. Figuratively knock on the doors of their minds and discover the valuable suggestions within.

The leader is responsible for pulling the best out of your people. Active listening, drawing out, and building common ground are essential skills to use. But pulling is not a one-time event. Success comes when you ask and keep on asking, seek and keep on seeking, and knock and keep on knocking. This is the way to receive, find, and have the door opened.

Lord, grant me the grace to ask others for their contribution and suggestions, the courage to tell others my views and opinions, and the wisdom to calibrate both push and pull. Amen.

Invested

A. Please identify your vital insight from this session and write it in your *Breakthrough* Journal.

B. For reflection or discussion:

1. For the following six skills, share your natural tendencies. Where are you naturally competent, and where do you struggle?
    a. Giving opinions and views
    b. Stating needs and wants
    c. Using incentive and pressure
    d. Active listening
    e. Drawing out
    f. Building common ground
2. Which of these six behaviors is the most significant learning opportunity for you?
3. What response plan or action items will help strengthen this skill?
4. Why is calibrating push and pull necessary in relationships and leadership?
5. What is your action item for this session?

49

The Performance Diagnostic

Invited

> *Now, LORD my God, you have made your servant king in place of my father David. But I am only a little child and do not know how to carry out my duties. Your servant is here among the people you have chosen, a great people, too numerous to count or number. So give your servant a discerning heart to govern your people and to distinguish between right and wrong. For who is able to govern this great people of yours?*
>
> *The Lord was pleased that Solomon had asked for this. So God said to him, "Since you have asked for this and not for long life or wealth for yourself, nor have asked for the death of your enemies but for discernment in administering justice, I will do what you have asked. I will give you a wise and discerning heart...*
>
> —1 Kings 3:7–12a NIV

King Solomon asks for a discerning heart and the ability to distinguish between right and wrong for his people and the nation. Discernment in administering justice benefits both the individual and the organization.

Determining how to generate superior performance is part of the leader's job. It is necessary to discern what factors contribute to the current reality. Whether we aim to fix a problem or reach a goal, four viewpoints can help us discern.

1. Has the organization clearly defined roles?
2. Has the leader provided appropriate training as well as support and challenge?
3. Does the individual have the competency for this set of responsibilities, or would they be better suited for another position?
4. Is the behavior in line with the organization's values?

Without discernment, it is all too easy to choose a quick fix that may completely miss the mark. Such a response satisfies the desire to do something but improves nothing.

Lord God, like Solomon, I ask you today for a discerning heart so I might administer justice in my relationships and responsibilities. Let me serve you, others, and my employer with wisdom and integrity. Amen.

Invincible

- Complete the Sherpa Training Session 49: Performance Diagnostic
- Video, 100 Exercise, and X Challenge

Involved

He has shown you, O mortal, what is good.
And what does the LORD require of you?
To act justly and to love mercy
and to walk humbly with your God.

—Micah 6:8 NIV

The prophet Micah presents three elements that help us determine what contributed to a team's or individual's dysfunction and what to do about it.

1. Act justly: consider what is appropriate under the circumstances.
2. Love mercy: show compassion or forgiveness where appropriate.
3. Walk humbly: choose meekness over arrogance.

These three qualities will serve us well as we determine the role of the organization, leader, head, or heart in the situation. They should also guide us as we create a response and accountability plan. What's more, the prophet declares these three attributes are good and are required of us by the Lord.

Lord, may I fulfill what is good and required of me. Let me deal with situations and people by acting justly, loving mercy, and walking humbly. Amen.

Invested

A. Please identify your vital insight from this session and write it in your *Breakthrough* Journal.

B. For reflection or discussion:

Use the Performance Diagnostic to consider how best to lead someone at work or home.

1. How well is the person currently performing? What improvement is expected?
2. Have their role and responsibilities been clearly communicated and understood?
3. Have they received appropriate training for their functions?
4. What measures of support or challenge might be helpful right now?
5. Do they possess the competency and capacity to perform this role?
6. Is there another role or function for which they are better suited?
7. Is their behavior in line with organizational or team values?
8. How might a discerning heart help you become a better leader?
9. What might be your learning opportunity: acting justly, loving mercy, or walking humbly?
10. What is your action item from this session?

50

CORE Process: Sherpa Training Takeaways

Invited

> *I have a special concern for you… leaders. I know what it's like to be a leader, in on Christ's sufferings as well as the coming glory. Here's my concern: that you care for God's flock with all the diligence of a shepherd. Not because you have to, but because you want to please God. Not calculating what you can get out of it, but acting spontaneously. Not bossily telling others what to do, but tenderly showing them the way.*
>
> —1 Peter 5:1–3 MSG

The challenge to "marry self-awareness to action" reveals a crucial reality for growth and change. We live in a world where we are bombarded with information on a moment-to-moment basis. And yes, some information creates "aha!" moments and insights. But without using the information on an ongoing basis, most of the potential benefits will be lost. We end up exposed to so many valuable and helpful principles but living few of them.

This final session of the Sherpa training is an opportunity to review and regroup. Review the contents of this yearlong program, and regroup by focusing on three current learning opportunities and your response plan with accountability to promote actions based on your insights.

In addition, consider framing the tools and principles of the GiANT content according to this brief admonition from the Apostle Peter. Here are the main points:

- Care for those you lead with the diligence of a shepherd, protecting them, providing for their needs, and tenderly showing them the way.
- Never use other people for your gain—define your success as building others up.
- You serve God when you serve others. Serving makes you a better person and is pleasing to God.

Lord Jesus, you are the Good Shepherd. We are the people of your pasture and the sheep of your hand. Thank you for taking us to your fields of joy and peace, near the streams of blessings. Your flock adores you because you always ensure we experience the best if we hear your voice and follow you. You seek what is lost and bring back what was driven away, bind up the broken, and strengthen the sick! You are my example and model to follow. Make me more like you and exemplify a good shepherd's traits, whether at home, at work, or in the community. Amen.

Invincible

- Complete the Sherpa Training Session 50: CORE Process: Sherpa Takeaways
- Video, 100 Exercise, and X Challenge

Involved

> *...your kingdom come, your will be done, on earth as it is in heaven.*
>
> —Matthew 6:10 NIV

When we practice Kingdom leadership (with a capital K), we are first acknowledging: I am *not* the King. I am not in charge. I am under the reign and authority of the King of heaven and earth. King Jesus!

One version of the Lord's Prayer phrases it like this.

> COME! Kingdom of God.
> BE DONE! Will of God.
> On earth (in my life and circumstances)
> as it is in Heaven!

The Kingdom of God is both the spiritual realm over which God reigns as king and the fulfillment on earth of God's will. A kingdom is a territory ruled by a king or a queen. Have you acknowledged the King of Kings as ruler over your life and how you exercise leadership (influence and authority) over others? Do you exhibit the reign of God over all that you influence (including self, family, your team, your organization, and your community connections)?

From Genesis to Revelation, the pages of the Bible sing forth that God is love. If this is true, then we must conclude God's Kingdom's primary characteristic is also love. While we speak about God's Kingdom coming into power, it is in the power of love by which God's Kingdom transforms the world.

Jesus described the priorities in God's Kingdom when he stated that the first and greatest commandment was "Love the Lord your God with all your heart and with all your soul and with all your mind." He quickly added the second most important thing: "Love your neighbor as yourself."

For the sake of Kingdom Leadership, we define love as: "Fighting for the highest possible good in the lives of those you lead."

Prayerfully consider a few questions as we conclude our Sherpa sessions:

- Have I asked Jesus to be King over my entire life and not a small "religious" piece in the corner?
- Do I ask Jesus every day to fill me with love to the brim so everyone who bumps into me today will get spilled on with the love of God?
- Will I let the Kingdom (the rule of God) be sovereign over my family, team, business practices, and all I touch?
- Do people look at me and see life under the authority of King Jesus? Do they see a life radiating the love of Jesus?

Becoming a Christian can happen in a moment. Becoming Christlike is the journey of a lifetime. This study is coming to an end, but we are on a lifelong journey together climbing to higher places. Theologically this is called sanctification. It is the process of the Spirit's ongoing work to transform our lives. We trust Jesus to lead us, strengthen us, transform us, and ultimately make us more like himself—the King of Love who is our shepherd.

Lord Jesus, open my mind to receive all you have for me in today's video sessions. Open my ears to hear your voice. Open my eyes to see where you want to take me—to the summit where I will behold the glories of your Kingdom. Amen.

Invested

A. Please identify your vital insight from this session and write it in your *Breakthrough* Journal.

B. For reflection or discussion:

1. What does it mean to make Jesus not only Savior but the King of your life?
2. How might things be different if you acknowledged God's Kingdom at your workplace?
3. What would change if vendors, customers, and employees were all treated as members of God's beloved creation?
4. What did you choose as your learning opportunity for *yourself*?
5. What are your planned response (action items) and execution (deadline and accountability)?
6. What did you choose as your learning opportunity for your *family*?
7. What are your planned response (action items) and execution (deadline and accountability)?
8. What did you choose as your learning opportunity for your *team/organization*?
9. What are your planned response (action items) and execution (deadline and accountability)?
10. How might your actions in these three areas give glory to the King of Kings?

Epilogue

Your Breakthrough Strategy

Invited

Congratulations on completing the GiANT Sherpa Training program! I trust you have sensed God at work and have reaped blessings for yourself, your family, and your team/organization.

People retain only a small percentage of what they read. Therefore, this course was designed for you to see, discuss, and *do* the principles we have been presenting.

It takes the *doing* to establish something in your life. Here is an idea for making our shared learning impact your life for years to come.

Please review all 51 of the vital insights you wrote in your Breakthrough Journal and sort them into groups.

- Group A: the concepts you successfully implemented that have become a valuable part of your thinking and living. Celebrate this success!
- Group B: principles and tools you want to revisit to meet specific current situations. Remember to consider all of the 5 Circles of Influence.
- Group C: principles and tools that would be helpful to share with others. How can you use

your knowledge to bless those in your family, your work team, and beyond?

- Group D: principles and tools that will require a plan for successful implementation. Use the CORE Process and write out your planned Response (action items) and Execution (deadline and accountability).

Working through each of these four groups of concepts will ensure you make the most of your newfound expertise. Now put a note in your calendar to repeat this process in three months.

Again, congratulations! I am so proud of you for completing this remarkable program.

Involved

Let me close our time together by blessing you in the name of the Lord.

May you grow in godliness carrying the Holy Scriptures in your heart and mind. May you experience abundant blessings in your daily walk with Christ.

> *For this reason, since the day we heard about you, we have not stopped praying for you. We continually ask God to fill you with the knowledge of his will through all the wisdom and understanding that the Spirit gives, so that you may live a life worthy of the Lord and please him in every way: bearing fruit in every good work, growing in the knowledge of God, being strengthened with all power according to his glorious might so that you may have great endurance and patience, and giving joyful thanks to the Father, who has qualified you to share in the inheritance of his holy people in the kingdom of light. For*

he has rescued us from the dominion of darkness and brought us into the kingdom of the Son he loves, in whom we have redemption, the forgiveness of sins.

—Colossians 1:9–14 NIV

May you prosper, and may the work of your hands be successful. May you experience God's provision in health, wisdom, finances, and family relationships. May you abide in righteous faith, trusting in the provision and love of our gracious God.

Blessed is the one
who does not walk in step with the wicked
or stand in the way that sinners take
or sit in the company of mockers,
but whose delight is in the law of the LORD,
and who meditates on his law day and night.
That person is like a tree planted by streams of water,
which yields its fruit in season
and whose leaf does not wither—
whatever they do prospers.

—Psalm 1:1–3 NIV

May the Lord guide and protect you when difficult circumstances come your way.

To you, LORD, I call;
you are my Rock,
do not turn a deaf ear to me.
For if you remain silent,
I will be like those who go down to the pit.
Hear my cry for mercy
as I call to you for help,
as I lift up my hands
toward your Most Holy Place. ...
Praise be to the LORD,
for he has heard my cry for mercy.

The LORD is my strength and my shield;
my heart trusts in him, and he helps me.
My heart leaps for joy,
and with my song I praise him.
The LORD is the strength of his people,
a fortress of salvation for his anointed one.
Save your people and bless your inheritance;
be their shepherd and carry them forever.

—Psalm 28:1–2, 6–9 NIV

May you walk in the power and authority of the Kingdom identity that God has given you and the call of God upon your life.

But you are a chosen people, a royal priesthood, a holy nation, God's special possession, that you may declare the praises of him who called you out of darkness into his wonderful light.

—1 Peter 2:9 NIV

May you experience God with you and within you every day of your life.

May the LORD bless you and take care of you;
May the LORD be kind and gracious to you;
May the LORD look on you with favor and give you peace.

—Numbers 6:24–26 GNT

In the name of God your Creator, Jesus your Savior, and the Holy Spirit your Sanctifier. Amen.

Index of GiANT Tools

Index of Bible Passages

www.ingramcontent.com/pod-product-compliance
Lightning Source LLC
Chambersburg PA
CBHW020150090426
42734CB00008B/768

* 9 7 8 1 9 5 4 9 4 3 0 3 2 *